I0145750

TWISTED CONSEQUENCES

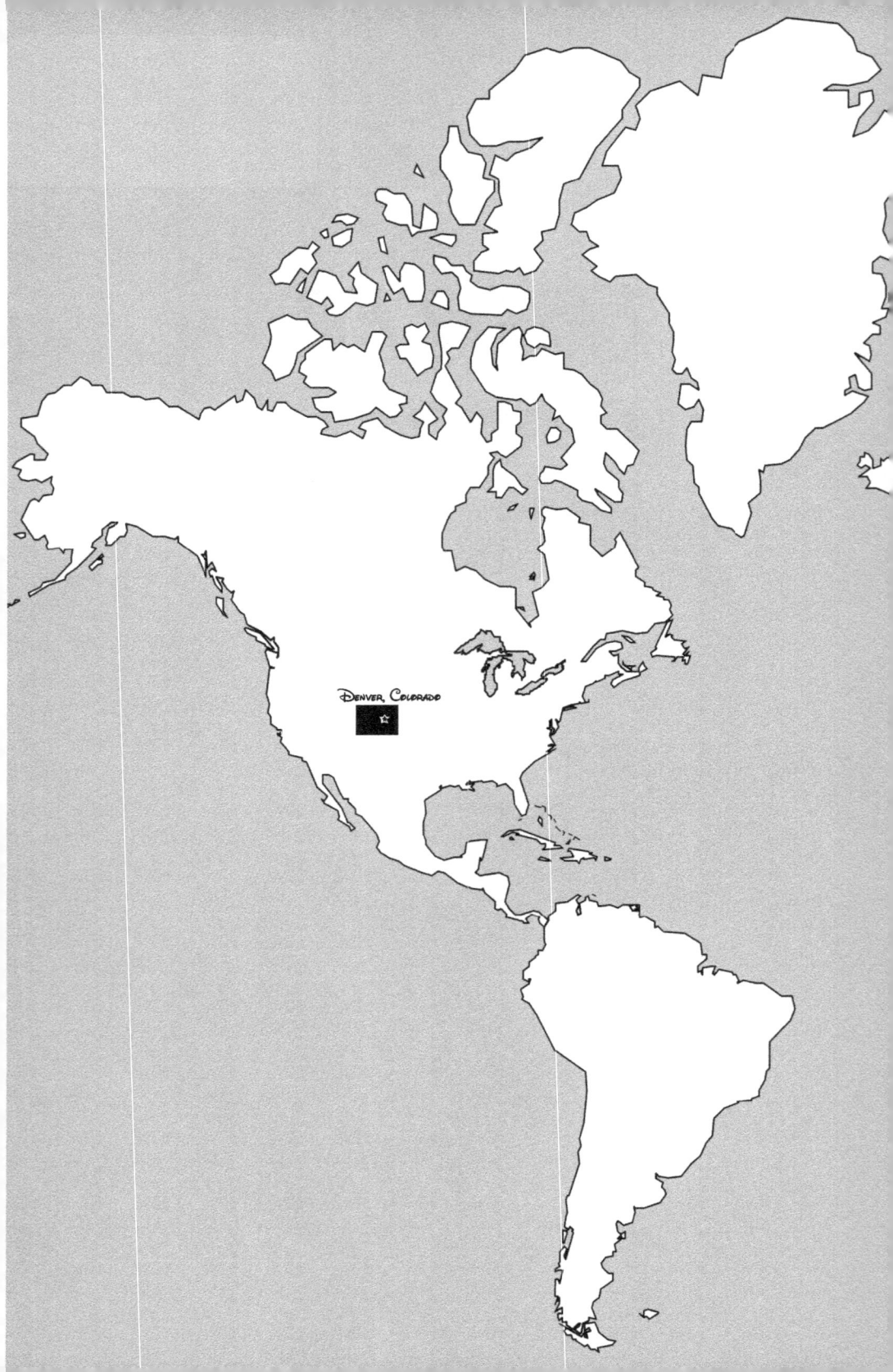

Denver, Colorado
☆

Bucharest, Romania

TWISTED CONSEQUENCES

IRIE PARKER

If you purchase this book without a cover you should be aware that this book may have been stolen and reported as "unsold and destroyed" to the publisher. In such case neither the author nor the publisher has received any payment for this "stripped book." Please purchase a hard-copy or PDF.

Copyright ©2008 by HendrickMedia, LLC.
All rights reserved.
Hendrick Media, LLC., Twisted@HendrickMedia.com
Printed in the United States of America
First printing: July 2008
Publisher's Cataloging-in-Publication Data
ISBN# 978-0-6152-3627-8
Book Design and text composition by H E N D R I C K M E D I A

Tis the business of little minds to shrink, but he whose heart is firm, and whose conscience approves his conduct, will pursue his principles unto death.

- Thomas Paine

CONTENTS

PROLOGE...............XI

PART ONE: THE RELATIONSHIP

1. DENVER, COLORADO...............1
2. NOVEMBER 1999...............7
3. DECEMBER 1999...............9
4. JANUARY 2000...............13
5. FEBRUARY 2000...............21
6. MARCH 2000...............27
7. APRIL 2000...............31
8. MAY 2000...............39
9. JUNE 2000...............49
10. JULY 2000...............59
11. AUGUST 2000...............63
12. SEPTEMBER 2000...............67
13. OCTOBER 2000...............73

PART TWO: THE JOURNEY

15. BUCHAREST, ROMANIA...............83
16. THE DECLINE...............95
17. THE CROSS...............103
18. THE ESCAPE..........109
19. HOME AT LAST.............123

PROLOGUE

In hindsight, it's easy to understand how the Internet has become a modern day "Pandora's Box." Since this new public technology was unleashed to the masses in the middle of the last decade, just a few years before the millennium, the Internet has changed the way some choose to live.

The people attracted to this phenomenon decided they were tired of going to the store for products which could be purchased through price comparison Internet portals. The pioneers of this medium realized the potential to automate ordinary, mundane tasks.

Many, for better or for worse, embraced this ideology and jumped in head first. For some, the goal of total automation combined with asynchronous communication became an addiction as complex as a virus.

Still, others were drawn into this web of illusion, based upon the impact of a powerful new human emotion, "cyberhope". This artificial paradise promised positive progress to mankind, with little or no mention of the possible pitfalls.

- Anonymous

PART ONE: THE RELATIONSHIP

I. DENVER, COLORADO

Greta, his loyal Rottweiler, could get her 20-foot retractable leash stretched out to the maximum. Doing this stopped her Tyrannosaurus Rex-shaped head about three feet from the sidewalk. A stranger seeing her for the first time would never guess Greta was a service dog donated to Tyson, the quadriplegic man who was working on his computer inside the house. Greta was smart enough to know that when Tyson was immersed in cyberspace, she was off the clock. Every morning Tyson would struggle to open the sliding glass door, slip the leash around the Rottweiler's massive head, and release her into the grassy common area. He would typically watch from the window, making sure the dog did her business, and then he would give the command she knew to return. This routine was ingrained in her extensive training, to minimize the amount of time the ferocious looking black dog had to cause trouble when tethered.

"Today it's warm. I'll let you stay out longer so you can sit in the sun, but Greta, you better be nice," he said in a serious tone.

The business line rang and Tyson rolled into his custom teak wood workstation. It was his ultimate escape, since this was cyberspace, where the playing field was equal. He delicately tapped the speaker phone button with the back of his hand. "Hello."

"Oh, yeah, I got your number on my pager this morning and-" The woman's voice sounded confused. "Um. Am I on a speaker phone?"

"Yes, you are." Tyson paused then cleared his throat. "I was calling because I looked at your web site again and was wondering if you'd be interested in doing a paid photo shoot. I have a client that likes your look and his pockets are deep. I was thinking maybe sometime next week."

He heard a car door slam shut, followed by Greta barking twice. He could see her reflection in the computer monitor. She had the leash maxed out.

"Oh, you're that photographer?" The woman squealed.

He couldn't believe she took so long to remember him, "Yeah, right! Remember I met you at that ad agency last week?"

Someone knocked three times hard on the office window. Tyson threw his arm on the desk, using only weak shoulder muscles, but still couldn't get his head around to look, and said in a direct voice "Listen, Tracy. That's your name, right?"

"Yeah"

The knocking increased to four hard slams on the window this time.

"I'm having a small problem here."

"What?" Tracy raised her voice.

"Hey, I need to call you back," Tyson said.

"Whatever!" She babbled, and then hung up on him.

He gingerly touched the button again to end the call. Tyson put the palms of his paralyzed hands on his chair's tires and sluggishly spun around. The knocker was the man known by all the neighbors as "Busy Body". He was always nosing around the neighborhood, with his undercover police officer looking mustache and oversized sunglasses. He was not afraid to approach anyone he considered to be in the wrong.

"Are you handicapped and deaf, too?" He shouted at the closed window. "Shut your damn dog up!"

"What the hell. No! Get the hell away from my window, geek!" Tyson yelled back. In his peripheral line of sight, he spotted Greta, sitting in the sunshine near the back door, unaware of the escalating situation near the office window.

Busy Body hit the window, "I said shut your damn dog up!"

"Who do you think you are? Some kind of vigilante?"

"No, but I'll call the cops!"

Due to the paralysis of his inner costal chest muscles, Tyson was losing his breath. "Get the hell away from my window, you freak!"

"Open your door, you little handicapped bastard!" Busy Body demanded.

"Allright, dude!" Tyson spun around, pointed his chair in the direction of the back door and pushed with all his strength.

In his younger years before his paralyzing car accident at age 21,

Tyson had taken many punches from schoolyard bullies, and he was never afraid to fight. Now he didn't even have the neurological control to make a fist. All he could do was bump into things with his light weight wheelchair. Aware of his limitations, he also knew that this guy would probably die in jail for assaulting a disabled man.

Tyson slowly rolled into position to slide the glass door open, and he observed Greta still relaxing in the sunshine. He wiggled his paralyzed knuckles under the door latch and put his shoulder to work. Twisting in a way that gave his biceps a certain uncontrolled muscle twitch, he provided enough force to break the seal and start the door sliding on its lubricated track. Greta looked in his direction and then got blind sided by Busy Body from behind, bulldozing her over and kicking at her. Tyson laughed while he watched. "This guy really is crazy," he said to himself.

The muscular black creature jumped up and made her instinctive lunge at the attacker's midsection. Snapping her jaws like a great white shark, she ripped an enormous hole in Busy Body's button-down shirt. He turned and stumbled across the grassy common area, looked back at Tyson and then limped up the redwood stairs to his sunning deck.

"Good girl Greta! Come! Now!" The leash made its loud recoiling sound, and her 150-pound body was promptly through the door. "Now we're going to have some fun," Tyson said to his beast. "Greta, kennel!" She darted into the three-foot by three-foot cage in the corner of the kitchen.

Tyson grabbed the cordless phone with the hand adapter on it, set it on his lap and then leaned back while pushing forward, creating enough of a wheelie to get the front caster wheels over the sliding glass door's threshold. He rolled into view of Busy Body's elevated deck, and just as he suspected, the man was looking down at Tyson, as he was yelling into his phone. Tyson slipped his hand into the adapted phone's handset, pressed it to his head, but didn't dial. He began barking orders into the dial tone. He wanted Busy Body to think he was pulling together a posse of friends to finish off Greta's work.

Tyson stayed out on his deck for several minutes. The fresh air felt good as he continued glaring at the idiot across the way. Suddenly, a jovial uniformed man appeared. He was grinning and shaking his head.

"Where's the Rott?"

Tyson pointed awkwardly with his limp fingers. "She's inside."

"You know it's illegal to tie a dog up in the common area." The animal control officer stated, while opening his metal clip board case.

"Oh, it is?" Tyson tried to sound surprised.

"Yep, any animal outside must be on a leash, and that leash must be in the hand of the registered owner."

"How am I supposed to let my service dog out to relieve herself?" Tyson flexed his normal functioning shoulders and biceps, enough to clearly demonstrate the paralysis in his wrists and fingers. Tyson looked for a reaction from the officer, while he noticed the man wore a hearing aid in his left ear.

"Well sir, that's not my problem now, is it? I'll need to see your driver's license!"

"Driver's license? Does it look like I can drive a damn car?" Tyson said enraged.

"Your Rottweiler's not registered with the city, and there have been some complaints concerning the animal's behavior. Any type of ID will do, sir."

Tyson held his tongue, stared down at his flaccid hands, and decided he couldn't pull the handicapped card on this guy. "Alright, will you help me get my wallet?"

"Sure sir." The officer sounded like a computer speaking.

"My ID's in the backpack," Tyson rotated his chair one hundred eighty degrees, exposing the black pack strapped to the backrest. He pretended not to see Busy Body doing some lame little dance steps up on his deck.

"Okay, you're ready to go," the officer said as he handed him the citation.

Trying to sound sarcastic, Tyson said "Wow, thanks dude."

Heading back inside, Tyson yelled "Eighty dollars! I better get back to work."

He gave Greta the command to exit her kennel and noticed the "new message" icon blinking in his office. Still fuming from getting the ticket, he propelled himself towards the office area. Tyson habitually spoke the words "retrieve e-mail" and the inbox showed a new written message had arrived while he was getting busted. When he saw it was from Michaela, his jaw dropped with excitement.

As far as Tyson was concerned, Michaela was his princess in need of rescue. They met through an on-line international dating service and had already corresponded three or four times. With all his stress temporarily purged, he began to read her message.

November 11th, 1999

Tyson, I am glad you wrote me and thanks for the e-mail. It is rather difficult for me to answer to you in time because my computer is out of order and I depend on one of my friends to send my e-mails. Tyson, thanks for attaching the drawing you made of that flower. It was beautiful and I really appreciate your work. As a matter of fact I admire you as a person because you have a strong character and will-power. Please allow me to give you some additional information about me. I am a student and I am attending the University of Foreign Languages. I speak English, Greek, a little bit French and Spanish, and of course, my native language, Romanian. I had some part-time jobs as a translator member of protocol stuff at different international forums and meetings.

I am cultured and I love to travel. I believe I am a strong person who understands the importance of being kind and tender. I consider I am very ambitious, eager to learn more and to improve what I know. Regarding my future plans I admit I am a little bit confused.

I imagine there is a huge difference between USA and Romania. Bucharest has a lot of old buildings and it is usually called "The Small Paris". It is a nice city but the most beautiful part of Romania is the country side. There, people are still practicing the old customs and it is incredible how simple their life is. Regarding the economic situation here, as you might know, everything is bad. There are a lot of people who hardly can live but on the other hand, the new generation, because of their technical knowledge, get easily a good paid job.

In Romania as in Russia are a lot of attractive girls but it is impossible to communicate with them because they are so narrow-minded. Most of them are going out with Turkish or Arab men only to buy them a few clothes.

Tyson, I will stop here, but not before I ask you to tell me some more about your country. I know from my best friend, who was in New York this year that everything is magnificent there. She says if I did not see United States it is just like I never saw anything.

When it was my birthday I was sad. I am disappointed because I am already 20 and I have not realized anything, yet. I would wish to do more things until now.

Write me soon and next time I will tell you about my family. I was about to forget. Please tell me about the treatments you follow. Many kisses for you,
Michaela Gogoasa

"I like this girl!" Tyson confirmed with a smile. "I'm going to meet her face to face if it's the last thing I ever do," he announced out loud.

Greta walked over and sat next to the wheelchair. She leisurely licked Tyson's lifeless left hand, bringing him back to his current surroundings.

"Good girl, Greta! What did I ever do to deserve such a good dog like you?" She looked up and seemed to have a smile on her snout. "Now I need to reply to Michaela's e-mail. Go get on your dog bed!"

Tyson and Michaela exchanged e-mails throughout the next eleven months which set the tone of their relationship. Tyson mastered the use of his voice recognition software during the process of getting to know Michaela. He would put his headset on and spend hours speaking into the microphone. Later, he would go back to the keyboard to clarify the content and correct any errors.

2, NOVEMBER 1999

November 12th, 1999

My dear Michaela,

I hope this message finds you well and happy. Thanks for taking the time to write. It's a pleasure to receive your e-mails. I have been very busy lately, I did four photo shoots this past week. Three were shoots for models' portfolios, which is the most fun work to do. From your pictures I think you would be a good model, what do you think? I've been doing some web site design lately, too. The money's better, but you can burn your eyes out looking at the computer monitor for all those hours.

Hopefully you're feeling better now. I was wondering what type of things you wish to be doing.

Okay Michaela, you asked about the treatments I follow. First I would like to say that my routine is fairly structured. I have a nurse that helps me get up in the morning, and also one that puts me in bed at night. The morning is much more involved and time-consuming than at night. It takes a good nurse an hour and a half to help me use the bathroom, take a shower, dress me and get me going for the day! I have been doing this a long time and I've accepted the fact that I will need to teach new people how to do this from time to time. The nurses come from an agency which I pay. It was hard to get used to at first, but now it's easy for me. The night routine usually takes an hour and is much easier. During that time I get in a standing frame which puts all my weight on my feet, and then the nurse straps six pound weights around my wrists. I do my physical therapist's prescribed weight lifting routine from this standing position.

Other than all this, I'm really independent! I believe this is the number one treatment to follow. A healthy independent mind can overcome anything. If I'm in my power wheelchair, I can do anything, like drive my van or cruise around outside the house. Well, enough about me for a minute. Tell me your opinions on sex and relationships. -Tyson

November 29th, 1999

Tyson,

It is a treat for me to read your e-mails. I had a bad week especially on Saturday when I was very upset that I could not even concentrate on writing you. You asked my opinion regarding sex.....MMMMM I think it is something normal. Most of the girls I know they have their on top regarding this subject and it does not matter who is the guy as long as they feel good. I must tell you I do not agree with them at all. Unless I am in love with someone, only then I would do anything to create pleasure. I must stop here because somebody presses me. How was the Thanksgiving holiday for you? Please tell me news about your work (and your models) and how you will spend the Christmas?

Tyson, I would like to call you once, of course, if you do not consider my proposal indecent. Michaela

November 29th, 1999

Michaela,

Thanksgiving Day went well. Everyone in my family behaved themselves. Ten people were here to eat and they all brought some food and cleaned up the kitchen afterwards.

I've been building a web site for a local punk rock band, and I'm getting prepared for a trip to San Diego to attend a design conference. Michaela, I'm glad you reminded me about Christmas, I almost forgot, I got so wrapped up in Thanksgiving I haven't even been thinking about Christmas yet. So, I have no plans.

I would love it if you would call me, and I would call that a decent proposal! I look forward to hearing your voice, or at least getting a voice mail. I had the clearest most vivid dream of my life last night, I was walking, not rolling, through a lush tropical forest with you by my side. -Tyson

3. DECEMBER 1999

December 7th, 1999

Tyson,

I am glad to get a message from you as usual but this time I am happier than before and I do not know the reason. Maybe because of this period of the year or, because somewhere, far away SOMEBODY DREAMT me...

Wow, the new photo you uploaded to the agency's web site is so nice, and Greta looks so good. By the way I bought one new dog, her name is Sheba, she is lovely and she looks like a doll. I would prefer also take a Rottweiler but I hardly can take care of a Canish (I suppose this is the English word)...

So, you will go to San Diego. I am glad you will not stay too long so you can answer my e-mail. I know, I am selfish.

In Romania it is difficult to obtain a visa. I am working for a Greek company and I went to the Greek Council to get a new one. The Counceller did not like too much my idea and she thought it was better not to give me it at all. For this reason I was appointed Director for Public Relation or Customers' Relations (I do not even know what exactly I am) to show to that lady I had an important position in the company. Some connections were also helpful and I obtained a six months visa to travel only in Europe to work.

Tyson, have you got a close friend? Tell me about the place where you are living, and the news about your work.

Ahh! I was about to forget. I tried to call you but I found out after I had to dial also 001 in front of your number. Is it correct? I hope you will excuse me for all my grammar mistakes because it is difficult to take the dictionary from home... Write me soon, Michaela

December 8th, 1999

Michaela, my Dear,

When I received your e-mail this morning it made me happy, too! Today I have been extremely busy. My partners and I are straining our brains trying to finish this web site. Even with the knowledge of all three people sometimes we don't know enough.

That's too bad that you're having a hard time getting a visa! Maybe one day after the New Year we could plan to meet somewhere in Europe.

I need to be honest with you right now. Can you be more specific when you ask me if I have a close friend? I think your question is important and I want to understand before I answer.

Well I do hope you try to call me again. I'm leaving early tomorrow morning for this design conference. So please wait until the week of the 12th. I'm not sure about the 001 but I will try to find out somehow.

Michaela, sorry to be brief, but I need to go. I'll tell you more about my living situation next time. Oh yeah, I almost forgot, did you get the roses I sent you?

Tyson

When Tyson returned from the conference in San Diego, the first thing on his mind was checking his e-mail. He found it odd that Michaela never replied. He didn't want to bug her, so he decided to wait for her to contact him. The hours dragged, and soon, the days turned into weeks. Tyson's excitement turned into mild depression, he couldn't shake this sudden loneliness. It had dawned on him at least twice, how strange it was, that this online relationship had him so emotionally upset. He figured he'd screwed everything up by sending such a romantic bouquet of red roses too early in the relationship.

On the fifteenth day of waiting, Tyson's phone rang exactly as his eyes were closing near midnight. His mouth was dry from the side effects of his muscle spasm medication.

"Hello," he said.

"Well, hello," a young woman's voice spoke in an innocent tone.

"Michaela, is that you?" His voice crackled from the dryness. Then suddenly his abdominal muscles contracted violently, forcing all the muscles in his left arm and hand to flex quickly. The unexpected spasm jerked the phone away from his head and slammed it against the bed's headboard. His weak grip loosened and the phone ended up spinning on the floor. Tyson's inability to rise to a sitting position caused this conversation to be over before it ever got started. He could hear her sweet voice coming from the floor, asking if he was okay a few times, then the line went dead.

Tyson decided to wait for an e-mail from her, so he could see what type of reaction she would have to this bizarre phone call.

December 20th, 1999

Hi Michaela!

Just a quick note to say thanks for the call, your voice is wonderful. I sometimes have a difficult time holding the phone when I'm lying down, that's why I dropped it. Sorry, Tyson

December 21st, 1999

Awww Tyson,

I was a little bit worried because you did not write me. I thought you were angry with me because I called you... I was so anxious to speak with you that I did not think that I could disturb your sleep, sorry.

Indeed, I received the roses but I was so surprised and I did not know how they reached here, of course, my mother lost somewhere the note. I imagined immediately you were the only person who could do it, but then I was afraid not to drop a brick. So, I decided it was better to let my mother to find the note to confirm to me I was right. My poor mother she looked for the note all these days and it was an occasion for her to clean the whole house. Yesterday I called her to find out the result and she confirmed it was you, she took Sheba to help her... It was so funny... Anyway, it is such a nice surprise, you can not imagine how happy I was. Thanks!

It happens to me to have some bad days but in those moments I am looking at your photos or I read some of your e-mails, the result is that I feel better. The photo you uploaded to the agency site from San Diego is pleasant. Did you manage to finish finally that web site? If you think you are a little bit tired after all these things just leave it. It is more important you to be ok.

These days I found out that tomorrow evening I would go to Greece. I was not surprised because I was expecting them to send me. I believe it will be nice because I have a lot of friends (half of the employees are Romanian who settled there).

I will come back on 28th and now I am a little bit upset because I know I will miss your e-mails and of course I will miss you. I will not have access to a computer with a modem in it in Greece. Please take care because I do not want to hear any bad news from you. I will miss you,
Michaela

December 23rd, 1999

Michaela,

I hope you have a merry Christmas in Greece. Thanks for the advice on just leaving the project alone for awhile when I'm tired of it! I also gain strength when I reread your e-mails and see your beautiful pictures. I will spend Christmas at my mom's house, it's about a 2 hour drive south of where I live. I'm quite worried about losing contact with you as some have predicted computer chaos when the calendar changes to 2000. Well, please write or call when you return from your business trip. I already can't wait and it's only the 23rd! I will miss you! Merry Xmas! -Tyson

4. JANUARY 2000

January 5th, 2000

Hi Tyson!

Greece was everything I expected, and I did some shopping, too. Hopefully nothing happened to your computer. No one in this country had their attention on this Y2K computer problem. We were told it was a made up story to push people into making unnecessary purchases.

I am anxious to hear how you spent the New Year's Eve. In Romania was great! It was a magnificent show in the center of Bucharest and the streets were full of people who were celebrating. I went with some friends to the World Plaza of Commerce which is the best hotel here, after the Hermes Opal hotel. It was great, everybody got tipsy before the midnight and it was a funny show watching how the others were staring at them. It was the first time in my life when I drank so much Champaign and I was not drunk in the next two minutes!!! Of course, I was tipsy, about 2 am we left to another party... and we froze half an hour in the car because of the snow. Finally, I came back home at 7 am when I watched on CNN the party from Times Square. I must admit it was an incredible show!!! You, the Americans, know how to draw the attention of the whole world!!! It was an opportunity to learn a few things about your people, too.

Tyson, I am still confused about my future. I am interested in a serious relationship but I do not want children. I like them very much, as a matter of fact I think is the most beautiful gift of a woman, but I simply can not see myself having one. Maybe you find my opinion weird, but I can not imagine myself with a big belly. I might want to adopt one, but it is too soon to think of this. You might say I am selfish and I do not blame you. I am confused about my professional life, I will tell you more about this later. I will stop here because I am going to buy something. It is a surprise. Take care, Michaela

January 11th, 2000

Hey Michaela,

Yes, New Years Eve is a magical time. I missed you!

I've been reading some research reports about the new techniques developed to fix central nervous system damage. The scientists have found a way to utilize the surplus of frozen fertilized eggs created during an "in vitro" procedure. This cell would have to be donated to science in the same way body organs are donated today. Usually the couple seeking the procedure will have twins or triplets on the first try. This is great, but it leaves around seven unused, five day old cells called blastocysts which are frozen and stored for future use. In most cases the last thing the couple wants is more children. At this point they will have the opportunity to help people with diabetes, parkinson's disease, central nervous system damage, and even alzheimer's. It's fantastic that, these couples who were previously unable to have one baby can now have as many as they choose. Then, when they're done having children they have a chance to make a difference in an existing life also. When I think about the history of mankind, I can't come up with anything more profound and noble than two people becoming donors. I believe they are calling this procedure stem cell therapy. It sounds cool. Apparently, the microscopic cell can be coerced into becoming any type of body cell. This could be the most humane thing ever done by human beings. Hundreds of thousands of people will suffer no more pain and agony. They are anticipating human clinical trials and FDA approval by the end of next year.

That's cool you got a husky. Is he a puppy? I'm doing well, but Greta is not. We are going to the doctor in a few minutes to have her foot looked at. I think she stepped on a thorn or a rock, or something sharp enough to puncture her paw.

Well I want to do some traveling, and I want to meet you! Do you have any desire to meet me? -Tyson

January 12th, 2000

Tyson,

The possibility of a central nervous system cure sounds great. I would love to meet you, could you imagine if you were able to walk up to me.

In February I will go to Cape Town. The company I am working for has another branch there and because of the political situation they want to close it and move to Romania. Even sick, last evening I had to go to meet an owner of apartments for the managers who will come here.

I am very restless because I have no time to study and very soon I will have some exams at the University. I must find a private teacher to improve my Spanish because otherwise I will not pass the exam. How is your work? Michaela

January 18th, 2000

Michaela-

Hi how are you? "Que Pasa?" Is my pathetic attempt at speaking Spanish. I think it means, "What's up."

I'm thrilled to know you would like to meet me! That's one of the great things I like about our relationship, the fact that we are both completely open and honest with each other.

This is just a short note to let you know I miss you! Also, I didn't see the third picture you posted until the other day. I like it! Your new dog looks good. I would guess he will grow as big as Greta!

-Tyson

January 21st, 2000

Tyson,

How are you? I am sorry it took so long to answer your e-mail but unfortunately the phone's bill was too high and I could not pay it in time. The line was cut and these days I stayed only in the house because I was sick.

Now, I am better. I had to study a little bit. I must say I hate to learn things by heart which I do not like or understand!

I would love to meet you! I do not think it will be a problem for you to come to Bucharest but I do not suggest you in this period of the year. It is very cold, around -10 or -15 degrees. I usually wear only short skirts but now I put on only pants. It is a tragedy! Write me soon. Take care, Michaela G.

January 22nd, 2000

Hi Michaela,

Now that was funny. Here I am reading your e-mail, waiting to hear bad news, and the tragedy is that you're wearing pants! It made me laugh. Thanks! I guess if I'm going to travel so far it would be best to wait until you're wearing short skirts.

I'm sending you a present for Valentines Day. It was a bit expensive, so I hope nobody tries to steal it in the mail.

Well, I've been preoccupied this past week with Greta. She was having problems walking, so we went to the doctor and he said the pain was in her neck. This appeared to be very serious. Sometimes when this breed gets older, the neck gets weak from the oversized head. The doctor prescribed a steroid used to reduce swelling in horses, and now she's doing better! I would be depressed for a long time if she had to be put to sleep. How's your puppy?

I hope you're dealing well with school stuff and your health. Write soon, -Tyson

January 24th, 2000

Tyson,

I am sorry to hear about Greta. Unfortunately I was so busy these days that I did not have time to take my dog to the doctor. I had to go last Friday and I did not manage till today. The weather is really bad here ... The snow has almost half a meter and some people even died in the mountains because of the cold.

I am so anxious to leave Romania, next Monday I might be in Cape Town. I was also to Johannesburg a year ago and it is beautiful. I remember that last year my suitcase was lost by the airline and when I reached to Cape Town everybody were staring at me because I weared boots and a thick coat, while outside was 27 C. Then I went shopping with a friend of mine and she was so ashamed to enter the shops with me that she started to tell to all the saleswomen why I was wearing boots. I am serious ...my winter clothes are about 13 short skirts and 4 half short (I don't know the English word) and only two pair of pants.

It is so nice of you to want to send me a present but believe me it is not necessary. What else have you done?
Hugs and kisses, Michaela

January 25th, 2000

Hey Michaela,

Wow, that's a funny story about losing your suitcase and wearing winter clothing in Africa. I also like to hear about your short skirts!

Well, Greta's doing better now. I think the steroids reduced the swelling in her neck area. Apparently this was all she needed. Now I'm getting a head cold, just feeling achy, and very out of it. You know what I mean? So if this e-mail seems different than usual, my cold is probably the reason. I have been busy doing more web site stuff for punk bands and getting ready to go to Miami... February 19th through the 26th, to be exact. Your travel plans sound exciting. I can't wait to hear the stories you tell when you return from Cape Town. -Tyson

January 27th, 2000

Tyson,

Your plans sound wonderful. I am also anxious to leave Bucharest, to get rid of this cold. I also take some photos in South Africa to send them to you. How long you will stay in Florida? I will be away one week. Of course, I will not forget you.

Ah, Tyson, I must be honest with you... I had an exam yesterday and I did not study at all. The teacher asked me a few questions and I told her the truth. Then she asked me what could I tell her about the French. I remembered I read once a book about how they were one of the dirtiest people during Ludovic the XIVth, they did not wash themselves, women were full of bugs and they used special forks to scratch under the wigs on their head. And so on, she did not like the story but she was very impressed because I knew it and she gave me a high mark. I was really lucky... Tell me about your nurse. Is she good?
Write me soon, Michaela

January 28th, 2000

Michaela,

Congratulations on your high mark. That's a very interesting story. When I was younger, I used to wish I lived during the medieval time. My teacher would tell me a similar story about women having bats living in their wigs and throwing raw sewage into the street! So, maybe it's better to be alive now.

That's great that we will both be going to warmer climates in February! I look forward to seeing photos from Africa. I will be going to Florida for one week this time. Usually, I go for two or three weeks, but my friend who is helping me can only get one week vacation from his work. So it will be a brief physical therapy session/vacation, but well worth it. I need the vacation and to get back concentrating positively on my body. It's weird how the mind can learn to ignore this paralysis. At the clinic in Miami, we work to improve my condition, even though the progress is minimal. I won't have access to the Internet, so naturally, I will miss you! I'm sending your present today. Hopefully it will find you in good health. Be Cool. -Tyson

5. FEBRUARY 2000

February 1st, 2000

Tyson,

I have only 5 minutes spare time and I could not help not to write you this e-mail. I still do not know if I leave today. They canceled the tickets and book other for tomorrow.

I am glad to hear that you are ok I hope to find time tomorrow to write you some more. Take care and be good while I will be gone... Can you promise me? -Michaela

February 1st, 2000

Michaela,

Sure, I can promise you! When I think about this it makes my stomach feel good! My stomach felt horrible when I logged on the internet this morning and read about this plane crash in Africa. I knew you were flying that direction today, and it made me panic! So it was good news to hear your trip got postponed until tomorrow.

I've been feeling a little restless lately. When I think about you, I feel better though!

Michaela, please have fun on your journey and stay away from plane wrecks! Be good! -Tyson

February 11th, 2000

Tyson,

Please do not be angry with me! I came back yesterday and I must tell you that visiting Cape Town was a good experience.

I have these days the exams at the University and I leave at 7 o'clock in the morning and I come back late in the evening I lost again about three kilos of weight only in two days ... My computer is still out of order and I must go down town to write you.. I am sending you this short message just to tell you I am still thinking about you! Lovely kisses from me I am so anxious to tell you about my trip... Michaela G.

February 12th, 2000

Hey Michaela,

It's really great to hear from you! It makes me feel good inside to know you're thinking about me! I was more worried than mad when you didn't write. I guess I didn't realize I'd become so attached to your attention. But, I confess, I am totally addicted to it!

That's good to hear you thought Cape Town was a worthwhile experience.

Lately I've been feeling strange, you know, like anxious, not really satisfied with my life as I've made it to be. One day I'll want to move closer to the city, where the majority of people my age live. Then I won't have to drive 75 miles per hour for 30 minutes to visit friends. On the other hand, I can't believe I'm thinking this way because I have built my environment exactly the way I wanted it. I don't know what's going on with me!

Wow, am I on a roll? I guess I'm just comfortable telling you anything and everything I'm thinking. Michaela, tell me more about what you did. Your lovely kisses are returned, but doubled!!! -Tyson

February 17th, 2000

Tyson,

As usual, first of all I apologize for my delay. Today I have ran until now to get the present you sent me. Unfortunately, I do not know Bucharest very well and I lost the way a few times. What can I say, I received many presents in my life but nobody succeeded to impress me like you!!!!!!!!! I do not know how to thank you, as a matter of fact

I do not find any words right now. I have never even looked at a digital camera and now I have my own. After I got the camera I ran home to bring some photos to scan them for you... This is the first thing I can do for you right now.

I hope that even if you find a new girlfriend or because of other reasons we can not e-mail each other some day, you must know that you will remain my friend for the whole life!!!

Do not be worried as long as you are thinking of me, nothing bad can happen. I feel restless and bored, especially because of the weather, it is so bad here. I have these kinds of moments quite often but then I start to study or read a book.

Tell me more about your house. The town where you live. My apartment is rather small but I feel so good there because it is mine.

You also should know that at your age you realized many things, things which maybe a 40 years old man did not understand yet... It happens also to me to be depressed sometimes and then I am thinking that things happen for a reason and finally everybody meets that person, whom they call soul mate, and who will change the life of the other person... For example, did you know that I did not write to this Agency? I had a relationship with a guy I broke up with him and I was bored... I had a friend, and he asked from me two photos ...telling me that he would solve my problem. I did not know what he did until I received those letters. After three months I saw for the first time this site and I was angry with him because he could choose some better photos!! So, you see Tyson, just because a friend of mine was enough crazy to help me not to get bored, I found you!

We have a saying in Romania. One minute can bring something that the whole year can not!!

You do not have to feel strange anymore. Even if it sounds like a cliché it is true. When you find a person and you will fall in love, things will change and you do not feel the same... It can happen even tomorrow, while you are driving in the street or it can happen in one year... It happens to everybody, maybe it is happening with us... There is another problem. When you choose to be with a person you must wonder if she is the best for you, too. -Michaela

February 18th, 2000

Michaela my dear,

Right now my stomach has this feeling again. It really intensifies when I see the online pictures of you and read your writing! I'm telling you, when I get your e-mail in the morning I'm powerful and completely balanced for the whole day!

This is difficult to put into words, and I didn't think this could happen through e-mail, but I'm quite sure that, well, you know, I'm guilty of loving you!!! I can't control it. It has hit me, I feel invincible and great. I hope this will not scare you away. Even if our eyes never meet, I'll always hold the idea of you close to my heart!

I'm glad you like your present. I thought it was perfect for our cyber relationship. Please show me your life. I want to feel like I'm there, and, of course, images of your lovely self will always make my heart beat quickly.

Well, I'm leaving for Florida on Saturday and won't have access to my e-mail account. Please write me soon so I can keep this good feeling going! I'll miss you!

When I return, I'm going to buy a second car that I can easily ride in as a passenger and have the driver put my manual wheelchair in back. I've been doing some extensive research and have it narrowed down to three sport utility vehicles. It's important to get the right height for lifting me into the seat and also have enough space in back. What's your favorite car, Michaela? -Tyson

February 19th, 2000

Ah, Tyson,

What a strange stomach you have got!! Mine, I believe, it is very small and unfortunately it suffers all day long because sometimes I forget to feed it... I am glad you like my photos... and especially that I manage to make you feel powerful. Every time I write you something it is what I really mean.

Your plans sound great. I do not know too many things about cars but I simply love them!! I drive a Grand Cherokee, which belongs to the company I work for, but I am trying to get my own car, too. For a woman, jeep or sport cars are the most suitable... I also drove once a Lincoln Navigator. It was incredible, that car was so huge.

I am so jealous of you. You will have a great time in Florida. Here all the days have been rainy lately. It is not cold anymore and next month is going to be spring. I am so anxious because I got bored to wear only pants!

Tyson, yesterday I took the digital camera you sent me to the office and the people gathered to find a solution how to use it. Most of them were girls so these kinds of things were totally unknown to them... It was so funny. You should be there to see their faces!!

Now I have got to go to the airport because another Greek is coming to Bucharest. Four months ago I went for the first time to wait at the airport for the Director of a big company from Greece. I did not know the way very well so I got lost and my boss was calling me every five minutes to ask me where I was. After one hour and a half I Finally reached to the office with the Director who was all in a sweat.

Please take care of yourself while you are left... I know there are a lot of girls there, so, try to be good! -Michaela

February 20th, 2000

Michaela,

That's great about showing your camera to your coworkers. I have a fun time showing people new technology and watching their jaw hit the floor and eyes bug out. It's like showing them an alien or something! Well I hope you get it working. My digicam is not as simple as the one I sent to you, and I admit it took me a few weeks to grasp all the concepts. It's similar to traditional photography in one way. You push a button to snap a shot but everything else is totally different! Since you're an intelligent young lady, I'm positive you'll get it figured out quickly. Let me know if you have questions.

Last night we got four inches of snow, so I'm even more excited to get to paradise and 80 degree temperatures of Miami. I've been comparing Bucharest weather to Colorado on my internet portal page for the past few months and we are surprisingly similar. Please inform me when you officially make the switch to short skirts so I can come visit.

I rented an Expedition on vacation once, which is comparable but not as luxurious as the Navigator. There are so many sport utilities out there, I could spend a lifetime trying to decide. I'm a Libra, you know the balancing scales symbol, and I've read we are notorious for being indecisive. For me, this is true most of the time!

Well, "guilty" might be a poor choice of words. I heard a song by a reggae band once where this phrase "guilty of loving you" was used. The lyrics in the song are actually a man talking to a woman. They appear to be just friends, and he is trying to express his deeper feelings for her by confessing with that phrase. I was trying to do that too. Sorry if it sounded a bit strange. Well, I'm curious if you think it's unlikely to fall in love through e-mail. I never thought it was possible, but now my strange stomach tells me different, I think! What do you think? Well, enough of my rambling. I need to start packing for my trip now. I promise you that I'll be a good boy!
Tyson

6, MARCH 2000

March 2nd, 2000

Tyson, welcome back, I would think you would be back from Florida today. I am so sorry. I was rather bad while you were left. Two days ago I had a new car accident. I think it is the first one this month... It seems that my car has something against the other cars on the road... It was not dangerous, but I had to pay a lot of money because of the damages... My car has not got even a spot.... One day before the accident I got my national driving license. I had an International one which I bought it (this must be our secret). This is the best thing in Romania, with money you can get everything here...

I liked your photos very much. You are so photogenic... Have you ever thought of becoming a model? I can be your Manager. We can make a lot of money. Trust me...

I was scheduled to go to Greece yesterday but they postponed the departure... On one hand I am glad because I can write you..... I am content because now I can concentrate on other things.

On Saturday I will go to my first Spanish class and when I will come back from Greece I will follow some Greek classes, too. I have to work hard. That is all... I am not angry with you because you left me here sad and lonely!!!!!!!!! Kisses, -Michaela

March 3rd, 2000

Michaela-

What's up crazy driver? You are careful when you drive, right? I don't want to sound like a daddy, but since I broke my neck in a car wreck, I understand what can happen when you're not concentrating on being careful behind the wheel! Speaking of cars, I'm now a new car owner as of yesterday. I decided on the millennium silver Toyota 4Runner Limited. When I get a picture I'll show you soon.

I'm glad you liked my pictures, and it makes me feel confident when you told me I'm photogenic! If you want to be my manager, that's fine. What did you do in Greece? I'm a little upset that I only received one e-mail from you between my trip and yours. Now I'm the sad and lonely one! I would love to hear your voice again in the night time. Can you make calls? Are you a religious person?

Well, I don't want to stop writing, but my webmaster job is calling, and I've already been working the computer all day. I'll be lonely until I hear from you again...

Bye Sweetheart, -Tyson

March 6th, 2000

Tyson,

Greece was interesting, and I have never had so much fun in my life these days... I met most of the Romanians and had a good time at all the week end parties.

Regarding our special relationship I have noticed that I am so open with you... Generally people describe me like a very cold person so now I found out that they were wrong... You know so many things about me and so do I ...it is wonderful.

I used to go to the church when I was a school girl every Sunday and I saw women there gossiping about the latest news. I think the religion is inside us. Your car sounds so lovely. I am very jealous of you....

Missing you a lot, Michaela G.

March 7th, 2000

Michaela,

That's great I made you feel better! Truthfully that's exactly what I want to do for you. Getting to know such a mature, honest, and intelligent young lady has brought me pleasures I have never experienced before!

I have read that Scorpio women are the most intense lovers, and that they are more comfortable when they are in control. Is this true for you? I have been in love once before my car accident and two times after. You know, the kind of mutual feeling that makes you glow all day, and even strangers on the street can see it on your face. All of these relationships had their flaws, which in the end destroyed the love. I would not trade this experience for anything in the world.

Communicating with you has definitely helped me rediscover my emotional, sensitive side, which I've chosen to hide for years. So, having said all that, I'd like to say, "Thanks for the inspiration!" Wow, I hope that wasn't too deep. Sometimes I get a thought in my head and I can't stop! But I feel close enough to tell you anything, and you're right, it's wonderful. -Tyson

March 18th, 2000

Tyson,

First of all you do not have to feel lonely because somewhere, far away, I suffer, too. You must take care of yourself and get well ... My best friend has just come from a tour of Europe and when she showed me what clothing she bought I went crazy with jealousy.... Here in Bucharest, it is snowing again and I simply hate this weather.

Please do not be angry, but the camera fell and now it is a hundred pieces... Tyson, please forgive me... Many hugs and kisses. -Michaela

March 29th, 2000

Hi Michaela,

Well my luck has been bad this month! This past weekend I was in the new Toyota going to a ski resort about six hours away. My brother, Jack, is in a punk rock band that played two shows up there and everyone except me went snowboarding. On the ride home, I got a little too comfortable in the leather seat and completely forgot to shift my weight around to keep my blood moving. Now I have two pressure sores on my butt and have orders from the doctor to lie in bed for a week, to keep all pressure off of it! However, I'm cheating, since I get up for one hour in the morning to pay bills and make sure everything is in order. I think about you often, and I've even tried to transfer that good feeling you make me have in my stomach to my sores for healing purposes. I'm not sure if that made sense, but you know what I'm saying!

Since that camera is really only an object, how could I possibly be angry? Please don't let that worry you. Sorry to be so brief. I miss you and hearing your voice again would be a great thing for me! -Tyson

7. APRIL 2000

April 3rd, 2000

Tyson,

I read your e-mails three days ago but I could not write you. I was so busy... I must solve some problems at the college because I want to study Italian instead of Spanish... My best friend came one month ago from Europe and she was very angry with me because I could not find time to meet her. The day after tomorrow I might go to Greece and she will not see me for another week ...I simply do not know what to do first.

I am so glad because you are feeling better... I have been thinking of you and I was really worried when I noticed you did not write me... In Bucharest the weather is very nice, around 20 degrees Celsius... It seems that very soon it is going to be summer ...I am anxious because on 17 of May I will get a new visa, I hope for the whole year. Please take care of you because I do not want to hear bad news anymore. Write me soon.... Many hugs and kisses, Michaela

April 7th, 2000

Michaela,

Hey, what's up Romanian girl? I hope this e-mail finds you happy and doing well. Did you manage to drop your Spanish classes? I can tell Spanish is not fun for you to learn! I must admit that I'm no good at learning any new languages. It's not that I'm narrow minded or lazy. My brain is much more visual than auditory. I have always been this way, even as a child. I will usually forget more than half of any new material I hear. However, if I'm trying to learn something that is presented to me visually, my comprehension is excellent, almost like photographic memory!

As you can probably tell I'm feeling much better. No bad news to report to you today. Actually, I feel wonderful and the sores have healed. Sometimes it takes something like having to stay in bed for ten, days for me to really appreciate the good things in my life. You know what I mean? Plus the weather is getting warmer and the days are longer now, so naturally this makes me feel better too.

I spent some time the other day looking at cruise ship trips. I wanted to find out if there are any that go to the Black Sea and Romania. It appears that one ship travels from Istanbul to Odessa and then to Constanta and Bulgaria. I am having problems finding when this tour occurs. I'm thinking it happens in late summer, like August or something. I don't even know if this is a good idea, but I want to let you know that I'm still thinking about meeting you someday. I really wish you could come and visit me. You would probably lose your head, if you saw the shopping situation around here.

I'm curious about your opinion on something. In your country, how do men treat women in general? Also, please describe how you think men should treat women. This is a very interesting topic to me, something I've been thinking about a lot lately. Well, I have to roll, so please take care and, of course, be cool! -Tyson

April 8th, 2000

Tyson,

I am glad to hear you are better and think more positive. I have given up my job because I must study hard for my exams... I have drop Spanish classes and attend the Italian ones... Italian is more useful here and I must find a private teacher to stimulate me.

It is going to be nice if you can come here but I do not understand why you want to come by ship and not by plane. I would love to come there but I do not know if I can get the Visa. If you want, I will try to find out which is the procedure.

I do not know how can I describe you how is a relationship here...I suppose it is the same everywhere or it depends on the partners. I want a man to respect me and I want him to be less selfish than I am.

I had a great time this weekend.... I will live for one week with my best friend because her boyfriend is away and she does not want to stay alone... We have discovered new places in Bucharest and we have a lot of fun... How did you spend the weekend? I will end my letter here and I wait for a new answer soon. Michaela

April 9th, 2000

Michaela,

It's good to hear you were able to find time to stay with your best friend. It's also good to know you managed to get rid of your dreaded Spanish class.

Yeah, the idea of visiting you by ship sounded like a good one at first. I was thinking it would be cool to see many cities in your part of the world. You know, get a good idea of what life is like in Eastern European cultures. Now I'm not so sure about this idea, because after talking with a travel agent, I learned this ship doesn't go to Romania. It doesn't sail until September, and it costs almost nine thousand US dollars. So now I need to work on a new plan. Also, I like the idea of you visiting America. There has to be a way! You should find out more about this procedure. I would love it. I'll do some research here too. I wonder if we could say you need a business visa to do modeling work for my photography business.

That relationship question I asked you was a tough one to answer. I think you're right about it depending on who the partners are. I believe respect is a big factor, along with compromise and trust. With these three things in a relationship, how could it be anything other than wonderful?

I don't think we have the same understanding of the word selfish, because you care about other people. I think this because you are always asking me how things are in my life, and you listen to my reply and try to help me with my problems. I have met extremely selfish people who don't even realize that things happen when they're not around.

Tomorrow I need to get up early to go to the hospital for my yearly checkup. It's basically a bunch of questions and people poking needles at me for three days. I'm not really looking forward to going, but

I know it's important for me to have these tests done. Please respond soon and be good.

   -Tyson

April 17th, 2000

Tyson,

   I am still staying with my best friend, somewhere near Bucharest, and it was rather difficult to connect on the Internet.

   It is a very beautiful place here...a huge garden and a lake...Today we might go on the lake by the power boats if it is not going to be cold...I am so relax and I feel that everything is perfect ... How are you? Have you done those tests? I went out with my friends and discovered a very nice place called Opium.....Opium is one of my favorite perfumes and may be that is why I liked it so much. What perfumes do you like? I am going now to "test" the weather because I need to get tan... I have got some new, hot, sweet kisses for you... -Michaela

April 18th, 2000

Michaela,

   Once again it's good to hear you're having fun in the sun. My favorite perfume is anything vanilla! I love that smell so much it can put me in a whole different world! I will go smell some Opium next time I'm at the mall. Tell me more about the place Opium. Is it a nightclub disco place?

   Well everything here is good, except my cat keeps getting into trouble. Now he's peeing on the next door neighbor's patio furniture and windows because they have a female cat inside. I don't know if I told you about my very expensive cat. His breed is called the Bengal Leopard, because they mix actual wild Asian leopard cat with other domestic breeds to produce a very athletic and intelligent toy leopard. The bad thing is he can be very territorial. So there are a few ways to trick him into not peeing over there, but the neighbors will need to help me do it. They don't want to help, it seems, but only complain every time it happens!

I want to make plans to meet you, Michaela! The way I see it, we could meet three ways. Either I visit Bucharest, you visit the USA, or we make arrangements to meet somewhere like a resort city in Europe. When I travel, I definitely have to bring someone, like my brother, with me. I want to know what you're thinking!
Tyson

April 23rd, 2000

Tyson,

How are you? What other bad things does your cat do? I have been on a trip in the mountains and I came back three hours ago.

I also must make some decisions regarding my future and I am very confused. Generally I always know what I want and I am able to do anything to get that thing... I might get a new job. And I do not know if I am ready to start working again. It is a great opportunity and usually these kinds of companies have the most well paid jobs. On the other hand I still want some more spare time to enjoy myself.

Well, In Romania, if you come, it will not be too much fun first of all because I do not know how often we can see especially if I start working again....It is also very difficult for me, almost impossible, to get a visa. I know that 40 journalists applied for a visa to go to NY and only three got it. In Romania most of the people prefer to buy it for $2,000 or $3,000 USD than to go to the Embassy. I still have a Visa to travel in Europe but it is going to expire on the 17th of May.

Opium is a bar and it looks wonderful...Everything is black and the music is great...I have not been there lately because it is always full and I must to book a table before I reach there. Which are your favorite places when do you go out? Thinking of you,
    -Michaela G.

April 24th, 2000

Michaela,

I'm doing well today but my bad cat brought me an Easter surprise yesterday morning. It was a large rabbit he caught outside! It turned into a huge mess, but everything is fine now.

Michaela, you are young and having time to enjoy yourself is important. Don't get so upset about your job decisions. Since I've known you it seems that you have no problem getting jobs. What is this new one?

Well, I've done some research on ways to get visas. The best I found is an international student visa, which takes forever to get and you need around $10,000 USD. So the way of buying your visa you told me about has me interested! I'm willing to pay for this and your travel expenses to visit me here. How does that sound to you? I think we should try this. I have never met someone like you, that's why I'm willing to send you this money via Western Union. There is a saying, "it's better to regret something you did than something you didn't do". That describes how I feel about this situation. -Tyson

April 27th, 2000

Good morning Tyson,

Even if it is 2:00 in the afternoon. I have slept like a log trying to recover the nights lost...It is incredible because I feel so relax knowing that I do not have to go to work early in the morning .. What are you usually doing in the evening? Before I used to come home at 8:00 pm watch a movie ,take a shower and then go to bed ... I couldn't go out because I was to tired ... What a bad cat you have got ...I bet that you spoil it so much if he does this kind of things . How did you spend the Easter? Do you have any customs? We have the Easter tomorrow ...and usually people here go to church on Friday ,Saturday and Sunday when they will eat a slice of bread called "paste" and eggs painted red. It is also forbidden to eat meat this week and do sins... I think I am a sinner because I have not respected any of these rules and besides this, tomorrow I will go at the seaside for four days. My parents do not know that instead of going to the church I will be in the Disco because otherwise they won't let me go.

Let us say I am a little bit surprise but very happy to hear your news. First of all give me some more information about this student visa. For how long is available and which is the procedure to get it. The money will be deposit in an account and they will give it back to you when I come back or this is the sum I must pay for the visa? I know other ways to buy a visa and it is cheaper than $10,000 USD. I wish very much to meet you but I also do not want you to spend so much money. I am waiting for these details and then we will see what the other possibilities are.

My sister is away for a few days and even if I was anxious at the beginning to get rid of her, I missed her very much. I was very upset when I had to give up that job but my sister and my best friend encouraged me all this time.
Many kisses, with the smell of vanilla. -Michaela

April 28th, 2000

Michaela,

Hey, great to hear you are feeling relaxed! Yes, last weekend was our Easter, and we have very similar customs as yours. It's funny because usually I get a chocolate bunny from someone, and then my cat brings a bloody bunny. It was a different kind of Easter at my house this year!

I'm glad my offer of meeting you here made you happy. Here are some details on the visa. First, if you have a high score on SAT test it's very possible to get a scholarship from a US university and a student visa (F-1 or J-1). If you have a degree already and speak fluent English, most state universities need international teaching assistants. I heard about some teaching assistants from China who can barely speak English, yet they get $9,400 a year from the university, a waiver of nonresident tuition and a student visa.

Of course, this would be more than a simple vacation. Who knows, you might enjoy being a student here. What do you think? I can certainly do more research on this idea! Please tell me more about the process of buying a visa.

Well, have a good four day vacation if you go....I can hardly see straight from the vanilla kisses. Wow!

-Tyson

8. MAY 2000

May 2nd, 2000

Tyson,

How are you handsome boy? It is good to hear so many news. I have been missing your e-mails all this time but now I am glad to write you again. How are you? I hope you are well. I did not have time to answer your letter because I left early in the morning. I had a good time and I got also tan a little bit. Yesterday I met the Ambassador of England and his wife and had the chance to see one of our ex-president's houses (Ceausescu - if this name tells you something). Anyway, I have just arrived and I am scared when I am thinking that from tomorrow I will have to study and solve also other problems.

I have talked with some friends regarding the Visa and I will have some answers very soon. Your way sounds the most secured but we will see. What is your opinion? Unfortunately I do not know what SAT test means. I attend a private college and generally the private ones do not give scholarships. I also know that I must send a letter to a college from USA and if they accept me as a student I also must prove that I have around $20,000 USD to pay at least the classes in the first year, so it is a little bit complicated.

I have noticed that your cat does a lot of crazy things ... My dog behaves the same but because I am not too much around her she loves more my mom and sister.

I enjoy smoking very much even if all my friends laugh at my cigarettes which are very slim and have no taste ... What do you smoke?

A visa costs here around $2,000 USD ...I do not know for how long, probably for a month. If I get one the second time if I apply for another one it is easier to get it. What do you think?

What kind of movies do you like? I will write you some more

tomorrow.... Did you have any serious relationship till now? If it is a personal question and if you do not want to answer me I will not mind.

Tyson, I am anxious to get a new letter from you. Take care, and I am happy because you liked my kisses,

Michaela

May 8th, 2000

Michaela,

I'm doing well, thanks for asking! I'm willing to pay that much for a visa. It would be great to have you visit for a month, because one week is too short. Are you still willing to come here? I think you should. What a great opportunity to experience this country, and meet me! Is this visa easy to get? How long will it take?

Yes I know how enjoyable cigarettes can be! I was smoking almost a pack a day in the last few years, but I've only had two in six months!

Well, I can watch almost any movie, but my favorite genres are action and science fiction.

I don't mind that question, it's important to communicate honestly about this topic though. I have been in four serious relationships and almost got married in the last one, which was two years ago. It's interesting that only one of these four relations was before my car accident. It was in high school and lasted three years until I moved away for college. What's your relationship background, if you don't mind telling? Ok, I have to go, but I'll continue to think of you all the time! -Tyson

May 9th, 2000

Tyson,

It is great to learn so many things about you. I had also a long term relationship which lasted one year and a half. I have never been in love and finally I decided to end it because I did not have enough freedom. I had a high way of living at that time and it was very difficult to go back to a normal life. All those things happened to me too early but I also realized that I got experience.

I want to meet you but I still can not imagine how it is going to be. Well, I do not know exactly how long is going to take, I believe around two weeks. I am not going to ask for one officially because I will not get it for sure and I can not risk. There are people who have connections and for a sum of money they can get it. This is how most of the Romanians go to USA. Of course, I must be very careful not to be cheated. A professor of mine can help me because she knows somebody who works at the Embassy or some friends who earn money doing only this kind of things.

How is the weather there? Here it is summer, over 28 degrees. I study almost all day long because in summer I have some exams and I must speak fluently Italian.

Which are your plans in the future? I ask myself sometimes what I am going to do and where I am going to be in five years but I do not know the answer. Do you think the destiny has the most important role in somebody's life? Tyson, if you find my questions boring, tell me. Kisses, -Michaela G.

May 11th, 2000

Michaela-

I'm sorry it took so long to reply. You were asking me very good questions, and I've been thinking about the answers over the past two days.

Well, Michaela, I am very anxious to meet you. So anxious that yesterday I wanted to quickly plan a trip to Bucharest for a few days just to see you. However, I didn't do it, because I started thinking it would be better to continue with the plan we've been talking about. Although this is a large amount of money, there is really no reason I can find to not get you this visa. This could be a life changing experience for both of us! I feel the money could not be spent in a better way. I need to know the procedure. Do you ask your professor friend first or do you need to have the money first? Also we need to find out how much airfare is from Bucharest to Denver. I've checked the prices from Denver to Bucharest and, depending on how much advance notice, the price goes from $400 to around $650. I'm guessing these numbers could be higher.

Your question about the future is a good one, but very challenging to answer. I'm sitting here looking at my computer, thinking about this, and here's my best answer. This is the way I see it. If I remain positive and deal with my day-to-day living in a responsible way, the future will take care of itself.

However, Michaela, I do think that destiny plays a huge role in all of our lives. You can't change it or understand it, but only notice that it's taking place. For example, in one year I collected over 100 addresses from this agency of women that I thought I could be compatible with. On the day I mailed my letters, I quickly looked at this web site one more time to see if I overlooked any girl. That was when I found you! I remember thinking to myself that I would be a very lucky and happy boy if this girl (you) had any interest in me. I did get a fair amount of replies from the 100 letters, but you are the only one I'm interested in. Therefore, I never wrote back to anyone else except you.

So, I don't know if this falls into the destiny category, but I think it comes close. I think I've found an educated and intelligent girl, that I'm comfortable telling my deepest thoughts, feelings and emotions to.

By the way, your questions are like your kisses, and they will never bore me! -Tyson

May 12th, 2000

Tyson,

Your last paragraph of your last e-mail makes me wonder if you really are interested in a relationship.... I know that most of those girls get married only to leave their country and to change their life's style.... They are so desperate to do it that they sacrifice their happiness. Well, I am not one of them!!! First of all, as you know it was not my idea to write to this agency. Later on, I was happy because I had the chance to know you. I also do not have financially problems and I enjoy living here. I have received proposals like this one before but I have never been tempted to leave Romania to meet somebody unknown. First of all because it is dangerous, then I could not leave Bucharest because my parents would never agree. I would say that I know you for a long time and I trust in you, that is why it was easier to accept. Now, I wonder if I should receive those money from you... I do not want you to have any doubts concerning my wish.

Well, that teacher will leave Bucharest at the end of the week. I have also talked to those people who do these kinds of things and they told me that I had to give them the money first. They also do not trust in anybody especially if they do not know the person very well. Finally they say that I can deposit the money in one account and they can not take them till the bank will have my approval. It does sound better than to give them the money at the beginning.

I have canceled all my plans to look for work this month because otherwise I could not leave Bucharest. I was interested in applying with a company that has just been opened and usually the first employees get the best positions. I wanted to get the job as soon as possible because I could have the chance to obtain also a car.

As soon as you will transfer the money I will find out all the details about the procedure.

I would say that I have asked myself many times what I will do in the future. I still do not know. Well, I will end my letter here. Take care.
-Michaela

May 18th, 2000

Michaela,

Wow, what a long day! I'm serious. I have been going at it since 6:00 am this morning. It's fun working all day, but I'm not used to this. Just today my old client called about shooting their annual golf tournament. Me, personally, I've never done this work before, but my business partner does this all the time. So we went down to talk money with them, and they gave us the job and wanted us to shoot this evening. So I just got done with this photo shoot and haven't even eaten all day!

I can't believe that I'm actually going to meet you!!! Also, I've been thinking that it's got to be tough for you to imagine how it's going to be. I think you'll have fun. Our communication is quite effective through e-mail, so why don't we assume that it'll be good in person. Everything will be just fine.

I did make it to the bank and wired you the full amount today, finally! It's scary carrying that much cash and you should see people's eyes when I roll up to do business with them. They can't believe a man in a wheelchair would have that much cash. It's really kind of funny.

You need to promise me you'll be careful when you get it. I worry about you, because I want to protect you, but I know you'll be fine. Okay, I have to go eat something. Your tracking code is MTCN#: 2982 -- 2704. You will need identification. Sweetheart, let me know how it goes. -Tyson

May 19th, 2000

Tyson,

I would say what a long night!!!! It is eight o'clock am here and I have not slept all night long ....I had an incredible time last night ...Some friends of mine took me out to a fashion show which was organized in a Disco ... At the beginning it was not exciting at all but after the show all my friends (the girls) were dancing on the tables while all the guys were staring at them ....I preferred to be good and they got upset ...Finally they convinced me to do the same thing. Because I did not want to spoil the atmosphere I did ... After a while the DJ said that one girl would be called the best dancer I still do not have the slightest idea why they chose me but I had fun when I started to tease the other girls... Later on we went to another Disco, the most popular in Bucharest, where other friends were waiting for us... Then we went to eat at the restaurant of another Disco and at 6 am in the morning we left to one club. It is like a ritual in Bucharest ...all the people after they leave different Discos, they gather in the morning at this club to dance again.

Tyson, it seems that you are very skilled and you know how to run your business ... Well it does not matter how much it takes to do your job...it is ok as long as you enjoy what you are doing... I would say that you are lucky because I still do not know what I would love to do... On the 17th my Visa expired and I was sad because I did not know when I was going to travel again ... Now I feel better especially because I am not going only to see a country but I am going to meet you, too. I hope you will not going to laugh of me but I really do not know how to proceed to get the money. It is the first time when I have to do this and I hope you will explain me.

I promise I will be careful although I am afraid that in Romania it is more dangerous than in USA ... Some gypsies attacked a friend in the middle of the day and stole from her a bracelet and a necklace. I might only have to transfer the money to another account ... I will know everything for sure very soon. Hugs and kisses from the distance,
-Michaela G.

May 23rd, 2000

Michaela,

I'm curious if you went to that bank yet. I've been waiting on getting your plane tickets, because we don't know the exact dates of travel yet. This is going to be exciting. I want to show you around our city. It would be excellent if you could stay a month. Will you do some modeling for me while you're here? I would guess you're good at it, since you beat all the other girls in the dance contest.
Tyson

May 24th, 2000

Tyson,

How are you today? I am a little bit sick and I have just spoken to my Italian teacher who was very upset because I canceled the appointment. I might change her because she is not so good. I have not been to the bank yet but I will go tomorrow. How is your city? How is the weather there? I would love to do modeling for you but I am sure I am not good for this. What kind of photos do you like to take? -Michaela

May 25th, 2000

Hey Michaela,

I'm doing fine this morning. Once again, I'm rushing around

trying to get things done. I hope you're feeling better, by the time you get this message. What are your symptoms? Please think of me and you'll be better!

It's amazing that I got up this morning thinking about how similar the temperature in Bucharest is to Denver. I don't really know why I was thinking about this, until I received your message asking me what the weather is like here. What can I say? Great minds think alike. Our community pool will be opening on Monday. It's really nice but I haven't been in it. Do you like to swim? Sometime this week I'll go and take a picture to show you how cool the pool is.

I think our city is a great place, and apparently lots of other people from out-of-town think so too. In the last 10 years, our population has increased more than most in the United States. It's a great place to live, because the Rocky Mountains are only an hour drive away. In the last five years with a good economy going, there has been more building than you can imagine.

Well, if you want to do modeling, you should, but if you don't want to, I would totally understand. I guess I asked you about that because, at the time, I was excited to be working in my studio again. Also, you mentioned that you won the best dancer competition at the disco. The photos I like to take are in good taste. I like to take a model and make her appear extremely sexy.

I need to go now because I've been experiencing a little bit of shoulder pain. Since I have an appointment to get an x-ray, I need to leave in five minutes.

Please be good to your self and always remember that I'm thinking about you. -Tyson

May 26th, 2000

Tyson,

You were right, I thought about you and felt better.

I love to swim … Last year when I was on vacation I learnt also how to take a dive… Unfortunately, the first time, when I tried to take a dive I thought I was about to drawn myself because I reached the bottom of the pool.

Somebody proposed me to take some photos for a magazine wearing a bathing suit. Although I was going to be very well paid, I could not accept... In South Africa some French photographers wanted to take some photos of me and I agreed but it was too late because we were going to leave the next day...

Tyson, it is a great feeling to know that somebody is really concerned about me. Is still paining your shoulder, I will massage it someday!

Yesterday I started working on the Visa, do not worry nothing can happen to me... The worst thing that those people can do to me is not to help me to get the visa or return the money ... But I know somebody who left Bucharest a few months ago helped by them so I am not worried ... I talked to them on the phone on Friday and said that they would try to help me but it is going to take a while because a few weeks before some Romanians went to NY and from 40 journalists only three got the visa ... Finally the Romanian press was very angry and they wrote some ugly articles about the Americans .. They gave the visa to the other 37 journalists and some of them didn't return.

Anyway, I am very optimistic. Tell me more about you. What have you done? Are you ok? I want very much to go to make gym because it is summer...

I have given up looking for a job if I come to visit you... Generally, it is very difficult to get holiday if I work. It is boring like this but I always find something to do. I think more often how it is going to be there and I still see everything like a dream...

I almost exasperated those guys calling them every two days about the Visa. I will stop here, it is very late but I had to come to see if there is any message from you. Tyson, write me soon. Many, many kisses.
-Michaela

9. JUNE 2000

June 6th, 2000

Michaela,

I'm also trying to visualize you actually being here, and I don't have a clue how it will be. I do have the feeling that it will be great and comforting to meet you Michaela!!! My plan is to do all my daily routine stuff just as I did today. I consider this to be my real job, stuff like managing the nurses and making sure my body, my house, and my pets are all taken care of. You know, basically, all the little repetitive things in life we all have to do to stay alive.

My situation is unique and frustrating because I have twice as many things to take care of than the average person does, and that average person sometimes believes that all I do is sit around and do nothing, while they have to go to work. Please don't think I'm complaining, because I'm not. Actually, I'm used to it now and it just gets easier with time.

Lately I've been trying to stay out of the heat, and I've noticed it's hotter in your city than here. It's interesting. I don't know for sure, but I'd guess Bucharest has that humid type of hot weather. Here we are one mile above sea level and there's no humidity at all really. When I was going to photography school in New York, I was amazed at the wet heat. It would make me mad when I was in class and started sweating out of nowhere.

I'm sorry to hear that you're bored from not working. You could occupy your time thinking about me. -Tyson

June 7th, 2000

Tyson glanced at the clock while rubbing his freshly opened eyes.

"Holy cow, who can be calling me at four o'clock in the morning," he mumbled while yawning. "Hello."

"Tyson, good evening," her voice had nothing but fear in it.

"Michaela, oh my God, is it you?"

"Yes it is."

"Wow, how cool! How are you?"

"I have some bad news and I do not want to scare you with an e-mail."

"What's wrong, Michaela?"

"I will explain to you the situation. After you sent me that money, because I did not trust in those people, I had to deposit it in a bank. Then they could take it only after I received the visa, because I planned on writing a check." She took a panic induced breath.

"Uh-huh," Tyson muttered.

"It was the safest way. If I was going to give it to them from the beginning, they could disappear with the money, with no way to know where I could find them."

"Yes, that makes sense to me."

"Everything was perfect because I only had to wait a little until they were going to get it."

"Well, it's good you're not carrying ten grand around with you," Tyson said as he raised his eyebrows for a second.

"Yes, I agree Tyson. During this time about four banks failed and they were declared broken," she said and then paused.

"No way, are you serious?" Tyson sounded furious.

"Yes, yesterday I was watching the TV and saw the crowd gathered in front of the government building protesting. This bank has blocked all the accounts of the investors. For the first time in my life, I do not know how to react."

"Calm down, sweetheart, your well being is more important than money! Is it safe to go out in the city?"

"No, it is a chaos in Romania because it is the fifth bank which was closed, and it is following another two. All the traffic is blocked in Bucharest, because people all over the country came here to protest and ask money from the Government. One man, a protester, was even killed today in the middle of the street. Many people, mostly the managers of these banks, were arrested. Over half a million people lost their money, and it is a tragedy here because the whole Romanian banking system has fallen," she sighed.

"Seriously, someone was killed over this?" Tyson said.

"Yes, and I was desperate all day long. I even missed one exam, because everything was so mixed up in my mind. I was afraid to write you, because I did not want you to have the wrong conclusions."

"Michaela, please don't be scared of me."

"Okay, Tyson, I feel better now because I am very optimistic, really. I will not need anything else from you. I will only tell you that I got the visa."

"What? Are you sure?"

"Yes, and I do not want you to think of bad things or not to write me again. Even if I do not manage to get the visa, meeting you is the main priority in my life. There are some countries where I can go without the visa or you could come to Bucharest."

"Will you need more money?" Tyson inquired.

"No! You sent me that money and I lost it. So it is my task to solve this problem alone. We are talking now about my pride and this kind of thing I cannot accept."

Suddenly, Michaela's voice sounded like she was under water. Then after three seconds, the line went dead.

June 8th, 2000

Michaela,

Well, sweetheart, at least you're honest ... I must say what a strange coincidence! Tell me what is happening? PLEASE BE CAREFUL.
Tyson

June 9th, 2000

Tyson,

I would not call this event a strange coincidence. It becomes something quite normal in Romania ... Well, I have watched the news and found out that this bank was not broken. The director of the bank declared that the money will be given back to the people at the end of July.

So, I have exaggerated a lot because I got panic immediately... Anyway, I am glad that everything is ok. Kisses,
-Michaela

June 11th, 2000

Michaela,

That is great news, what a scary situation, though! I looked at CNN's web site and saw one picture of a bank with many protestors and fire and what appeared to be some military soldiers.

It makes me feel better when you tell me not to worry! I will admit that I was extremely upset when I heard about this failure. All of a sudden, I was thinking I'd never get the opportunity to meet you, but now I've relaxed and I'm once again excited about our plan. With the bank problem going on, do you think these guys can still provide the magic visa?

I've been trying to stay busy lately and it's working. Last Friday, I went to one of my friend's (who's getting married next week) bachelor party golf tournament. I don't play golf, but I have fun driving my power wheelchair around the course and doing some off road four wheeling. Last night I went to a CD release party for my brother's band. That was fun because I've been involved with parts of the process of making this CD and what a relief it is to be done.

Today I'm resting, because tomorrow we are shooting a golf tournament with 144 people playing. My partner and I will have to be quick. We are going to get the group shot and all the individual golfer shots at the first hole, and then we'll rush to the lab and wait for them to develop the pictures. After that, we'll go back to the golf course with the photos ready to be handed out as they finish the game.

On Tuesday, I'll be going to another seminar all day for training on the new software from Adobe.

What have you been doing? I hope this letter made sense because I can hardly concentrate after receiving your lovely kisses. I don't want to sound greedy, but I wish I could have at least 1000 more, no make that 2000 more! -Tyson

June 13th, 2000

Tyson,

I feel really great...especially after that episode... I am roller skating with my friends and I stopped to write you something ... I am glad you are relaxed now and because you are convinced that I was telling you the truth.... It will not be any problem to get the visa later on ...On August it might be possible to change even the system...that means the Romanian might not need a visa to travel in Europe ...This will be wonderful but it is hard to believe it because most of the population will leave the country.

Your business seems to be very successful...I wish I could find something interesting to do...it is boring not to do anything... I have some problems with my exams...Last month I got the transfer to study Italian ...Unfortunately my knowledge must be at the same level with the knowledge of my colleagues... It is difficult to learn it in one month even if I have a private teacher... I must pass around 7 exams and I do not think I will.

I really feel good, I have been going to make a gym lately.... It is summer and I must be careful with my body. I would send you anything you want ...even more than 2000 kisses! -Michaela

June 14th, 2000

Hey,

That makes me excited! I think in America women sometimes make men get excited by accident or possibly on purpose. Then when the man advances, she gets mad, "because I thought you were my friend," cries out her mouth. My point, I guess, is that I'm already friends with you and we have a stable commitment feeling developing. I think its great, don't you? This feeling is real and not some little shallow minded game which people play in clubs or discos. You know what I'm saying? You can tell me things like sending me more than 2000 kisses, and I can freely say that every time my mind starts to imagine the passion my stomach spins out of control and all I can do is sit here and smile!

We did the photography for the golf tournament, and it was so hot and took so long that I was close to being dehydrated. Since we were working and had to do this quickly, I really was being stupid not to stop and cover myself with water and sunscreen. I always believe experience is the best teacher.

How did your exam go? I know it's difficult to do it, but you're smart and if you do fail, it won't be from lack of intelligence. Good Luck!

I'm happy the bank situation is solved. Now we can proceed with the plan. I'm curious what your parents think. Sit tight and be cool.
-Tyson

June 21st, 2000

Tyson,

How are you sweet boy? I always miss "talking to you". Last night I was happy because Romania football team played versus England and won the game...In Bucharest at 2 am all the people were in the street celebrating...I forgot my phone in a friend's car which was parked down town and could not sleep all night because I thought they stole it... The circulation was blocked and I had to walk to reach there.

I am with some friends at my best friend's house and watch films ...It is wonderful... We are waiting for another girl to come and then we will go out.

I would love you to call me but unfortunately you can reach me only on the cell phone and it is very expensive ... My sister will go on holiday soon to Antalya with her boyfriend and I do envy her... I wish I could see you sooner. How are you? Miss you, Michaela

June 24th, 2000

Hey Michaela,

I just tried to call the cell number, but you didn't answer. So I tried to leave a message for you. Did you get it? If you don't mind, I'd like to call again. What's a good time? If I call at 9:00 am here, I think its evening in Bucharest. How was your weekend? Missing you! -Tyson

June 26th, 2000

What a pity....I have no idea why my cellular was switched off....You can call me anytime ...even in the night...it won't be any problem.... I did not get your message...Be careful when you dial the number.

Today I went to the gym and took my father's car...when I left I saw that the tiles or tires (I don't know how to spell it) of the car were cut by somebody with a knife...My father was not so happy when he heard.

It was ok on weekend ...I had a fight with my best friend ...We have not spoken to each other for a few days ... But finally tonight we went out and discussed like two mature girls.... Now we will watch a film, she says it is very good. What about you? What is going on there? Missing you more.
-Michaela

June 27th, 2000

Hi sweetie,

I tried to call ten times yesterday and the day before. I called ten more times today. I even switched some numbers around to see if that worked, but a busy signal is all I got.

So, what did your father say about his car? It really wasn't your fault, was it?

On Sunday, Jack and his girlfriend picked me up and we drove to visit relatives at my mother's house. It was fun, and I wished you were there too. I really want to get you on the phone, even if it's just to say hi and hear your lovely voice again, Michaela. Let's keep trying. -Tyson

June 30th, 2000

Hi, Tyson,

I have been waiting for your phone call all these days. The number listed on the dating web site is my number, and I do not understand why it does not work. Maybe the numbers you dial in front are not correct.

Are you close to your brother? My sister has been left for nine days and I miss her a lot. I have not got too much time to think of her because all I know is Italian, I even dream this language, but in the evening when I realize she is not there to talk to her I feel lonely, especially because I could not speak even to you. I attend those Italian classes almost everyday and it simply kills me because I must pass those exams and that means I must know the whole language by heart. I am stressed because I do not know if I can succeed to learn it in two months.

My father is still angry and he says that if I want him to forgive me I must go to see my grandmother. He has been trying to convince me for six months and I did not want to go... This time I could not refuse him after what I did. So I will go on Monday and I will stay there a few days. What else? ...I gained a little bit weight last month and I did not eat at all last week ... I was about to fall down once when I tried to stand up... I was worried but at least I got my weight back down. It is a

bad weather here, I do not feel like doing anything ...only to be somewhere far away ... Maybe to a place called Denver?

Sometimes I do regret that I do not work because now I miss a lot
of things ...I have not been away for a long time, I miss my colleagues
and besides this I depend on my parents financially. On one hand I just
hope that something will happen, maybe when I see you I will not feel
so lost. Kisses and many hugs, -Michaela

10. JULY 2000

July 6th, 2000

Hey Michaela,

So, how was your visit with your grandma? Has your father completely forgiven you now? I had a good time at my friend's barbecue Fourth of July party. I had to come home early because I did something bad. I smoked a cigarette! Believe me, this was a terrible idea. I got very dizzy and I also turned pale and green. I felt like I was going to throw up. You know how it feels, I'm sure. When you're not used to having nicotine in your blood, it can make you sick as hell. Other than that, I had a fairly relaxing Fourth of July weekend.

Well, that's all the news around here, except for today I have to take my cat to the veterinarian because he's sick and won't eat. Speaking of that, how is your health doing? I'll be talking to you soon.
Missing you, Tyson

July 8th, 2000

Hi Tyson,

I came back two days ago from my grandma's... All my friends did not recognize me because I changed a lot ... I dyed my hair. I am reddish now. It is an interesting color and I look like a French girl especially due to the hair cut. I will leave this color for a while but I will dye my hair blonde again because I can not get used to my new look.

Well you should not try to smoke again if that gets you dizzy. I also smoke some slim cigarettes which look like small sticks ... They are tasteless and I believe less dangerous than the others.

I have seen on CNN how you celebrated the Independence Day... It was interesting. I hope to hear you soon. Take care. Kisses. -Michaela

July 12th, 2000

MICHAELA,

I've been wanting to sit here alone and concentrate on writing you an e-mail, but it seems like someone has been looking over my shoulder every minute of the last week. Please don't think I'm making up excuses. I'm just trying to be honest with you.

Well, have a good day and think of me when you need strength. It works for me to think of you this way. -Tyson

July 13th, 2000

Tyson,

I was not angry with you because you did not write, I was simply worried. I also read your e-mails and sometimes, later on, I answer back... I think of what you say, I analyze the words ... I think I should consider myself a very lucky because I have found somebody like you ....I have felt great reading your letters ...I felt the same when I got your present. I did not expect and it was a nice surprise to discover that you could trust in me... I do want to meet you, and I also know that this will happen ...If I was not interested in you I would not write you.... To tell you the truth, I do not write you so often because I go to check my e-mails only when I must write you back.

They have arrested some new executive members of the bank. I know that in USA if such a thing happens the Government is obliged to give the money back to the people. In Romania it is not the same. As a matter of fact regarding this bank an institution of the state called CEC guarantees the security of the money... It is a long story ... The bank where the account was is called FNI (The Fund of National Investments)

My best friend will go tomorrow for a month and a half to Monte Carlo...I am very sad because I am the only one who remains in Bucharest...All the others are going somewhere to spend the rest of the summer.

I have lost also a lot of weight because I don't eat...Yesterday, I ate only two eggs and in the evening when I went to play tennis I was about to fall down...What do you think? Kisses, -Michaela G.

July 20th, 2000

Hey Michaela,

Thanks for your lovely e-mail. When you tell me about not eating, why not? Its good for you and, with your intelligence level, you should know this. Well that's all I'll say about it, because I'm also a believer in not trying to change how people act or think. Instead, we should learn and grow together.

My brother, Jack, and I went to see a concert on Saturday at a natural amphitheater in the mountains called "Red Rocks". This place is great because they put everyone in wheelchairs in the front row. It got a little scary though because a few times some kids tried to get on stage and nearly knocked me over! Overall, it was a fun time.

What would you say if I told you that I have an opportunity to visit you in August for 5 days? I know our first plan is not completely dead, but I'm just thinking of the other options. My brother, Jack, has some time off and a passport. So I want to know what you think.

Tyson

July 31st, 2000

Tyson,

I am sorry for this long delay.....Believe me I had a very well-grounded and also delicate reason not to write you...Since I have not been working I had to depend on my family financially.... (Thing that I hate the most) Last week I had a fight with my father and as punishment he decided to cut all my expenses ...So, I was very unhappy and stayed only at home. To show him that I was not affected at all, after two days he regretted but I refused to accept his support ... So, tomorrow I will go to a casting to get a part time job. It is about advertising different products. I hope I will get it. Anyway, I will tell you more about it. I think it will be great if you can come to Bucharest. ...I mean it is wonderful... I will be free all the month, I have no exams till the end of the month. All I want is you to hurry up, I am anxious to hear more about it ... Write me soon, all the details. If there is any information which can help you, let me know. Billions of kisses,

    -Michaela

II, AUGUST 2000

August 2nd, 2000

Michaela,

Good to hear from you finally. I really was worried about you and this also put me in a bad mood.

Well, since I sent you the e-mail about visiting Romania in August, some things have changed. Let me explain the situation. The only person I know that has a passport and also understands everything about my medical condition is my younger brother, Jack. So I asked him in July if he would be willing to travel after he completed his college exams. He only has ten days before school starts again. I told him about you and our relationship, and he was excited to go. So then I called and made some plane reservations to Bucharest. I didn't pay, because I needed to communicate with you first. The airline gave me something like seven days to call back and pay. So then I began to play the waiting game. Time passed and the reservations expired.

Then my brother called me last week to tell me that his band has been hired to play the second stage at the Xgames in San Francisco in the middle of August. He told me that he possibly could leave school for a week in late September or a week in October. So that's the story right now. I'm sitting here frustrated, because all I want to do is meet you in person. We have both put lots of time, energy and money into this relationship, and I will die before I give up!! I really wish you were here, and we were going to the Xgames this month. Now tell me how much fun that would be!

I also need to tell you that in my research on traveling to Bucharest, I've found that visiting your city is something people in wheelchairs don't really do often. I contacted 20 travel agents on the Internet who advertise their services especially for wheelchair travelers to destinations worldwide. I typed out a few sentences explaining the situation and also asked if they had experience in setting up travel plans for people like me to go to Bucharest. Only one agent said he would help me, and that he set up a trip for someone five years ago to Bucharest. He said to be prepared for the accessibility to be scarce. Since my brother and I are a good team when traveling, this comment does not frighten me.

Before I start planning a trip with this agent, I need to know your current feelings on our original plan. Do you think the phony visa thing could still happen? If not, I will make arrangements to come there. -Tyson

August 7th, 2000

Tyson,

I am so disappointed because you can not come this summer!! Do you think it is still possible to come at least on September or October? It will not be a problem for me ... I have been trying to talk to my best friend about the Visa...She is not in Romania but she will come at the end of this month. There is still a hope.... I will try at least to get Shengen Visa (to travel around Europe) if it is easier for you.

All my friends have left to the seaside ....I am the only one who is still in Bucharest. I have been trying to study but I could not concentrate since you have written me about your possible arrival...I read your e-mail a few days ago but I decided to write you back only today...I wanted to tell you some good news. Hugs, millions of hugs.
-Michaela

August 9th, 2000

Tyson saved a couple hundred bucks, with the intention of spending it all on a one hour phone conversation with Michaela. He felt the surprise call would be a good tactic to bring some spontaneity to their slow moving relationship. He glanced at the clock. Since its 9:00 am. here, it's got to be early evening there, he thought. Tyson began dialing the seemingly endless amount of numbers with the palm of his hand into his modified phone with large buttons. Once he heard the line ringing, he tapped the speaker phone button and waited for an answer.

"Buna." Her voice was quick, quiet, and remarkably clear.

"Hey Michaela, it's Tyson."

It took her a second "Oh, really?" She said in an excited whisper.

"Yeah, it's me," he replied in a confident tone. "How are you?"

Still using her low voice, she said, "I'm in the theatre." There was a five second pause and then a squeaky door could be heard opening and then closing. "Tyson, what a surprise. I did not know you would call me," Michaela said in her well-pronounced English accent.

"I wanted to surprise you, sorry if I interrupted."

"No, please call me at any time, its good to hear your voice." She sighed and giggled with happiness.

"What theatre are you at?" Tyson said politely.

There was another long pause, followed by some loud static. She said something and the pleasing accent unexpectedly sounded like a female robot. The bot rattled off a few sentences of gibberish, and then all Tyson could hear was a busy signal. He repeated the dialing process multiple times, only to hear the same sound every time.

August 18th, 2000

Tyson,

I have no ideas why our phone conversations keep being interrupted, do you? I am happy to know that finally I am going to meet you...In October will not be a problem ...Tell me more about this ... I will have some exams very soon and have to pass all of them. Tell me more about you and how life is out there? Missing you a lot. -Michaela G.

August 29th, 2000

Michaela,

Hi sweet girl. How are you? I've been keeping myself extremely busy since our latest "under water" phone conversation. It was great to

66

hear your voice. I've been doing more research on coming to Bucharest. What is the rental car situation like there? Usually when I travel, we rent a 4-wheel drive vehicle because it's easier to get me in and out of. I really, really, really, miss you!
Tyson

August 30th, 2000

Tyson,

I have been very busy studying for the exams. I go to college every day and I spend my evenings with my best friend who has just returned from Monaco. I have been so happy to see and talk to her. She has brought me some presents, too so, my week was almost perfect.

I have also been trying to talk to some people to get the Shengen Visa because it is depressing to stay only here... I hope that finally she will help me. I am glad you keep on searching how to come here, if there is anything you want to know just ask me. You can rent any type of car you want here... I think you can do it even through the Internet because I have understood that these rental companies are all over the world. The weather is getting colder and I do not like it at all. I can't believe that actually we will meet ...I am very happy and anxious in the same time. I just hope that you truly want this. Thousands of kisses,
Michaela

August 31st, 2000

Hey Michaela,

Have you been to the Crowne Plaza Hotel Bucharest? I'm also looking at the Inter Continental and Hermes Opal. Of course, I truly want this. Please tell me why I wouldn't. Remember, I would do anything just to meet you. Your kisses are so sweet!
Millions more back to you,
Tyson

12, SEPTEMBER 2000

September 4th, 2000

Tyson,

I am happy to hear this good news...I went only to a party on the New Year's Eve to Crowne Plaza hotel. And it is nice. I have heard also that the Hermes Opal hotel is the best and it is located on the center of Bucharest.

I am curious to find out all your plans...Who'll come with you? How long do you want to stay? When do you plan to come? Taking into consideration that it is the first time when you come here I believe that you need all my attention... If you are a little bit worried that you travel to a foreign country well, I think that you should not be concerned because there are many foreigners who live or work here and some of them are Americans. You can get anything you need, as a matter of fact things are cheaper than in America. I know that in USA you usually pay through credit cards which can be used also here.

I am just a little bit sad because I wish that we could meet somewhere else, so our date could be an experience for me, too. Unfortunately I do not think I can get that Shengen Visa very soon so I can travel to countries like Hungary, Turkey... So, what do you feel regarding this meeting? I still can not believe that it really will happen after all we have been through.

Tyson, I hope you will write me soon... I will try to write you back also as soon as possible. I go daily to college because I will have some exams this week. Appreciating your millions of kisses,

-Michaela

September 6th, 2000

Yes Michaela!

This looks like it's finally going to work. I've been working on this trip for three days and have some solid plans. I'm coming with my brother and sister, and I'm sure you will like them. Jack is 26 and Diana is 22. They both know how to take care of me in traveling situations. I'm extremely happy that they are available to help me on this journey.

We will land in Bucharest on Air France flight 1888 at 1:45 pm on October 19th and leave at 7:00 am on the 25th. I have made reservations for two rooms at the Hermes Opal for six nights. One room is guaranteed to be handicap accessible. I also reserved a Mercedes van from a rental car company. We don't have this vehicle in the US, but I saw a picture on the internet and I believe it will work. So will you meet us at the airport and help us get to the Hermes Opal hotel? I'm so excited and very anxious. It will be a great thing!

Can't wait to see you,

Tyson

September 6th, 2000

Wow.....Tyson,

I can not believe that, actually, next month I am going to see you....I am happy and scared in the same time because I do not want you to be disappointed.

I think it is better if your sister and brother will come with you... What do they say? How did you convince them? It seems that you do not really need any help, probably also while you will be here because I have noticed that you can easily manage by yourself if you have planned everything so fast. I suppose that here at the airport you will have to pay a tax of 33 dollars to get the visa, that is all. I would like to wait for you at the airport. Tell me more..... Kisses, -Michaela

September 9th, 2000

Michaela,

Yes I know the feeling of happiness combined with nervousness. Whenever I think about next month, traveling into a foreign country and of course meeting you, the excitement is overwhelming. I try not to imagine exactly how things will be because when I do this, it sets me up for disappointment. So what I've learned to do in situations like this is to expect nothing and just do it with a positive attitude and then there are no worries. Does that make sense?

My brother and sister seem to be excited, too. They are both graduating from college in December. So, to answer your question, it was easy to convince them.

I should tell you now that they really don't know very much about our relationship. Of course, they know about you, but they have never read any of our e-mails.

I know I did plan everything fast, but, when I get there, I believe I will still need your help. Actually, I think it will be fun if you can show us around your city and even other parts of Romania, too. Since we will have the rented van, do you think we can go see castles, Transylvania, and the Black Sea? I would also like to spend some time alone with you. Tell me what you're thinking.
Kisses returned,
Tyson

September 15th, 2000

Tyson,

You should not be worried ...I have read your e-mail long time ago but because I have been staying with my best friend lately (she hates to stay alone) I tried to write you back but I could not connect to the Internet.

I think it will be an interesting experience for your brother and sister to see this part of Europe. Here life, somehow, it is different.

I just hope it is going to be a warm weather. Usually it is cold so bring with you some thick clothes. Now, the weather is nice but on October usually it rains. It is a good idea that you rented that vehicle ... I do not know how it is like to drive in my city.... For me it is something usual because for one year and a half I used to drive every day. There are not many accidents but some drivers are really crazy. Anyway, if you, your sister or brother do not want to drive I can do it.

Well, I do not know how it is going to be when we will meet...I can not even imagine ...somehow it is unusual but also very exciting. Do you want me to wait for you at the airport or it is going to be somebody who will drive that car there to pick you up?

I have just finished my exams ...this is the end of the second year. On October it is the beginning of the third year... My sister is very happy because it is the first year when she starts studying Law.

Now it is your turn to tell me about your plans ... Kisses ...till I will see you, -Michaela

September 23rd, 2000

Hey Michaela,

How are you? I'm getting excited to travel soon. I agree with you about our meeting being unusual, but, at the same time, I can hardly wait. I will also be nervous. I've been thinking about meeting at the airport, but I'm starting to believe that it would be better if we meet at the Hermes Opal hotel, which would be more private with less confusion. You know how it is to land in a foreign country. I think once we are at the Hermes Opal, it will be a much more comfortable and relaxing place to meet. What do you think about this?

I reserved a rental car and will be picking it up at the airport. There is really no way I'll be doing the driving, so I'll most likely have my brother Jack do it. How far is the Opal hotel from the airport?
Many more kisses back to you,
Tyson

September 27th, 2000

Tyson,

I am also very anxious regarding your arrival ...and I agree with you. It is better not to meet at the airport. The hotel is located downtown and it takes around 20 minutes to reach there. Will you be able to call me when you will arrive? You can call me from the hotel and dial only the number without the country code. Do not forget to bring thick clothes and a jacket. I still can not believe that it really going to happen... Maybe we can take some photos when you will be here ...After I have seen this photo of you online, I wonder who is going to be the model, you or me. What have you done at that design conference? It seems that you have been busy? Do you still work with models? I have passed all the exams and on the first of October I will start the third year of study. Fortunately I do not have to go daily to college. I also go every four days to that Italian class and I am trying to learn the language by myself, too. Of course it is a torture because except my teacher nobody else speaks the language so I can practice. Have you been watching the Olympic Games? I will stop here and hope to hear news from you soon. -Michaela

13. OCTOBER 2000

October 2nd, 2000

Michaela,

Thanks for the happiness! It's still working and life is good. Your comment about me being a model is well taken, but I think you would have more potential than me!

Last week's design conference was interesting. I got to learn all the latest cutting edge stuff on internet web site developing. Some day I'd like to start a business doing this stuff, if I can find the right partner.

Now here's some bad news. My sister was in a car accident last week. It wasn't that bad, but she has to wear a neck brace until Wednesday, when she'll go to the specialist doctor. So she may not be going to Romania, but we'll know more on Wednesday.

Yes, I tried to watch the Olympics as much as possible. I watched half of women's gymnastics and cheered for your country. I wondered what the reaction was like in Romania when that girl lost her medal for taking cold medicine? I also watched the swimming and track events. What did you think about the Olympics?

Well, my birthday was great. One of my friends is a driver for a limousine company, and he got one of those Hummer military vehicles that was stretched into a 14 passenger limousine. I went out with about 8 people to some night clubs around town. It was fun, but somewhere along the way, all of a sudden it became REALLY fun. This must have been when I received your sweet kiss! -Tyson

October 8th, 2000

Tyson logged in to his news delivery Internet portal. This was the first thing he did every morning. He subscribed to this particular site because it was rich with customized content. His favorite feature was the site's ability to analyze every piece of data on his hard drive and retrieve any relative news articles off the Internet. Today there was only one match. His jaw dropped when he saw that the search found the words "Michaela Gogoasa". He clicked on the link and saw her name surrounded by Romanian words he did not understand.

*Trei tineri aflati au plonjat de pe faleza constanteana in mare Gavril Dragomir, de 18 ani, impreuna cu prietenul sau Pavel Mironescu si **Michaela Gogoasa** se plimbau sambata, dis-de-dimineata, cu autoturismul marca Cielo prin Constanta. Cei trei au ajuns si pe faleza Cazino din orasul de la malul marii. Conducand cu viteza, Gavril Dragomir nu a vazut ca se apropie de curba pe care faleza o face in dreptul cladirii Statului Major al Fortelor Navale si a lovit balustrada de metal care a cedat. Apoi, autoturismul cu cei trei tineri la bord a plonjat in mare. Norocul celor trei a fost ca adancimea era de circa 1 - 1,5 m. Incidentul a fost observat de soldatii aflati in garda la SMFN. Un sergent si doi soldati au coborat cu ajutorul unei parame si i-au scos pe cei trei din autoturism. Din fericire, victimele nu au avut decat cateva contuzii. In schimb, autoturismul Cielo este avariat in proportie de 80 la suta.*

Tyson needed to do a rough translation, so he opened another web browser window and slowly typed the URL for the linguistic translator site. He spent the rest of his day typing in one Romanian word at a time then copying the translated English word into his word processor. His translation read as follows:

"Three youths plunged down the sea cliff. Gavril Dragomir, age 18, together with his friends Pavel Mironescu and Michaela Gogoasa herself, drove Saturday at dawn through the safety barrier. Those three very wealthy youths were leaving the cliff casino near the town of

Constanza. Caused by speeding, Gavril Dragomir, not an experienced driver, was turning to the right of the building of the naval forces and hit the metal barrier which was about to fall. Then, the automobile, with three youths on board, fell into the sea. They were lucky that the depth was about 1 to 1.5 meters. The incident had been observed by the soldiers who were on guard at the naval installation. The sergeant and two soldiers descended, with the help of one ferry, and took the three from the car. Happily, the victims didn't have any injuries. However, the car is 80 percent totaled."

After reading the story, Tyson was very confused and upset. He was unsure about the correct strategy to use. He felt it needed to include a quick confronting e-mailed question asking if she had been involved in this accident. Also, he wanted her to translate it, so he could compare it to his crude version.

October 9th, 2000

Michaela,

I've attached a news story I found on the Internet. Please read it and tell me what you think. You and this girl have the same name. Was it you? What does this news story translate to in English? -Tyson

October 10th, 2000

Tyson,

That accident happened in Constanza which is a town located near Bucharest. Fortunately none of those persons were hurt ... I am glad you had a good time on your birthday. It is a special day when you are allowed to do whatever you want. Even to get drunk. I was counting the days yesterday and I could not believe that in a few days you actually would be here... What are your parents saying? Your friends? I am sure that the only problem is to find to do something everyday... I will go to sleep now. It is very late but I had to reply to you because tomorrow morning I will leave my friends house and go home. Many hugs, -Michaela Gogoasa

Tyson sighed when he read and noticed that Michaela was very brief and never really came out and said it wasn't her. He was not happy with this lack of information. He occupied the next ten hours by infiltrating a Russian mail order bride internet newsgroup. Posting the article along with some details about their relationship, netted five responses from various Romanian speaking members.

The collective decision by popular opinion was that it most likely wasn't her, because the name "Michaela Gogoasa" was as common as "John Smith" was in the United States. So, in order not to disrupt the new relationship, he chose not to challenge her nonchalant response.

October 11, 2000

Michaela,

Wow, what a scary accident. You should have seen how worried I was when I saw your name with that article! You could even ask Greta. I freaked out!

Now I'm getting prepared to travel. Which is about three times the amount of work than it takes the average person. There are things I'll have to bring that I don't necessarily need, unless there's an emergency. I need to be prepared for anything concerning my medical condition.

My parents admire the courage it takes to fly across the planet and stay in a foreign country. So you could say they're happy about this journey. When my friends ask "Why Romania?" All I do is smile and say, "Why Not?" -Tyson

October 12th, 2000

Tyson,

I am a little bit nervous when I am thinking of your arrival. I do not know how I will react when I am going to see you and I do not know which will be your opinion about me. I am also worried because I do not know what we can do here. I do not want you to get bored. What else do I feel? Well, I am counting the days ... My sister is also very anxious and she asks me if I have news from you every day. I think that is all ... Michaela

October 13th, 2000

Michaela,

I think this nervousness is a natural feeling, because I'm feeling it here, too. Please just be yourself and I'll do the same. I have the feeling that it will be awkward for both of us at first. So we really can't worry about it, but I think we'll be happy to see each other.

I don't care what you do, as long as it's real. You might turn and run, or even better, jump on me and hug and kiss me. What ever feels right at the moment!

I'd like to get to our hotel and get situated, and then give you a call. Would you have a way to get to the Hermes Opal hotel? In my mind I'd prefer that we can meet privately at first, probably in the hotel room. How does this plan sound to you? I think too much planning can ruin something.

So, this is all I'll say. "I'm counting the days also."
-Tyson

October 14th, 2000

Tyson,

Just like you I prefer not to make plans. Well, the truth is that I do not like hotels at all. In Bucharest I only know where they are located. If you want to see me before I can come to your room and I hope I can manage to find you. You will have to tell me the number first. Well, you will notice that in the beginning I am a little bit shy but this happens only till I adjust myself.
-Michaela

October 16th, 2000

Michaela

I started to get nervous when I watched the news today and saw the terrorist attack on the USS Cole Navy ship off the coast of Yemen.

I also get a little nervous before I travel anywhere. So the best way for me to get rid of the nervousness is to find something to do. I think I'll try to go out and visit some friends.

I'm really so excited to see a place I've never been and, of course, I can't stop thinking about meeting you!

I hope you feel better, see you soon babe! -Tyson

PART TWO: THE JOURNEY

15. BUCHAREST, ROMANIA

Without hesitation, Tyson formed the disabled person's dream team in less than one week. Pulling his brother, Jack, out of college for seven days was easy. His skills in travel and nursing abilities were unmatched by anyone walking with a passport. Rex was hired to replace their sister, Diana, who was still bothered by minor injuries from her car accident. Rex's history was relatively unknown, but his size alone made him an easy choice to hire as the group's bodyguard. Tyson had met Rex a few times at local rock shows over the years, but the two never did much talking. The dark-skinned, golden gloves boxing champion made the team seem invincible. Tyson paid a large sum of money to land Rex in Bucharest two hours before the brothers' flight hit the ground. Since Tyson did not know what to expect, he wanted Rex to watch for anything suspicious at the gate where he and Jack would exit their plane.

Tyson assembled the group for a meeting ten hours before Rex's flight left, and he stressed the importance of treating the journey more like an undercover military mission than a European vacation. He delicately reminded them that they were both being paid to do what he asked and not to trust anyone other than him.

The landing gear deployed, and the tires skidded onto the runway, as they touched down at the Bucharest Otopeni International airport. Tyson was bothered by the stench of hot rubber blended with brake dust. The airplane slowed to a standstill, and the pilot turned off the seat belt sign. The passengers started moving, swirling their body odors around, which increased the potency of the smell. The three flight attendants moved up the aisle like cats stalking their prey. From behind they could have been triplets, with identical 5'8" body frames dressed in tight-fitting, peach-colored flight suits. They turned to instruct the passengers, and it was apparent they were unrelated, since each had her own unique facial features. When they spoke the

Romanian language, it was unlike anything the Americans had ever heard. Tyson found the sound of their words to be so beautiful, like the song of the first bird to arrive in spring.

This was no ordinary day for two reasons. Tyson found himself on the other side of the earth on October 19th, exactly ten years to the day after his terrible car accident in 1990. The other was that he was finally going to get to meet Michaela in the flesh.

Rex was the first human the brothers could see as they crossed the bridge leading from the plane into the modern Bucharest Otopeni International airport facility. He was pacing around, carelessly blocking the view of a crowd of locals, who were silently waiting for their acquaintances to exit the aircraft. Rex was clearly not concerned about blending in with the native people or looking for anything precarious. Instead, he stuck out like a sore thumb. He was wearing an oversized red, white and orange striped sweater. A large pair of green glittery sunglasses covered his eyes and cheek bones, and a bright red cowboy hat, with the words "Don't Mess with Texas" embroidered in white, sat on his husky head. Jack pushed Tyson towards the baggage claim, and Rex slowed his pace so the exhausted brothers could keep up. That's when Tyson noticed the snakeskin cowboy boots Rex was wearing.

"Dude, weren't you supposed to dress inconspicuously?" Tyson muttered in a soft voice. "Did you bring any clothes that make you less noticeable? I already draw enough attention to our group. We don't need any more."

Later, after successfully retrieving their baggage, Rex turned around and lowered his own bag to the floor.

"I brought mostly black stuff, see?" In his gargantuan fist, he held some black socks and a charcoal colored silk shirt. "Check this out guys." He stashed the clothing and pulled out around a dozen little plastic souvenir statues from his pants' pockets. "These are all famous landmarks in Paris. I got them at the newsstand there at Charles de Gaulle International, while I waited for the connecting flight to Bucharest." He crouched down to the marble floor and tried to reconstruct the city with the landmarks in the correct locations.

Tyson spotted an overweight man sitting on the other side of the baggage claim area. He appeared to be reading a magazine while moving his head slightly up and down and side to side while turning pages.

His eyes were fixed on the three of them. Tyson acted like he hadn't noticed this man and placed his attention back on the plastic statues on the floor.

"Come on dudes. I'm already feeling jet lag. Let's get our rental car before I pass out." Tyson demanded.

Somehow they all agreed to focus on getting to the rental car area. Jack spoke confidently with the rental company's representative to obtain the keys. The seven passenger Mercedes van had been confirmed weeks in advance. They loaded their gear into what seemed to be a moving advertisement for the local rental company. This was not what Tyson was thinking of when he made the reservation.

With half-open eyes, he commanded, "Alright, let's find this Hermes Opal hotel. I'm seriously getting tired."

"Me too" Jack acknowledged.

"Well, give me the keys," Rex said. "I'll do all the driving if you want." Rex dropped his shoulder and lifted Tyson's little paralyzed body into the front passenger seat, and then he placed his red cowboy hat on Tyson's head. "Cheer up, little buddy. I'll get us there. No problem."

Rex snagged the light weight wheelchair with one hand and stacked it with the luggage in the back of the van. Jack curled up in the back seat and closed his eyes. Within minutes, he began snoring.

Everyone waiting at the bus stop nearby stared at the odd-looking vehicle, covered with orange logos. Rex slowly released the clutch, and the Mercedes in a clown suit rolled out of the rental car pickup area. Rex honked the horn twice and waved at the dozen emotionless, frozen faces.

"Arrivederci!" He shouted out the window. No one moved or even blinked. The crowd resembled a herd of deer frozen in the headlights of a speeding automobile.

Tyson tipped the cowboy hat back and snickered at Rex's ignorance.

"Dude, you just yelled goodbye in Italian."

A few minutes later, they found themselves stuck in a colossal traffic jam. There didn't seem to be any stop lights or laws for driving. The rude motorists appeared to rule the road. The surface of the street was severely damaged, and the grooves between the cobble stones and all the pot holes were partially packed with sand. The further they drove the more war-torn structures they saw. It was evident that there had been no reconstruction efforts for over ten years, and the city was in shambles. It was also obvious that traveling on foot was more efficient than driving a car.

Tyson heard some type of heavy transportation rolling on a track a few blocks in front of them. All the cars caught up in the congestion braked to a stop, even the ones with impolite operators. An old, badly rusted yellow trolley car came chugging around the corner, spewing clouds of thick, black diesel exhaust into the air. The seating in the trolley car itself was completely full, and forty or fifty dark-skinned people dressed in black leather attire were standing, tightly gripping the overhead metal bar. This huge piece of rolling machinery easily dwarfed the cars and moved like a gigantic dinosaur through the intersection. Tyson could now be filed into the delirious category, he thought to himself. He looked up at the giant trolley overhead and spotted a heavy duty marine rope hanging from the metal piece attaching the car to the wiring above. The tar-soaked rope looked extremely hazardous. The smell was so pungent that Tyson's eyes shut tight for a few seconds. As the trolley rolled through the intersection, his gaze turned to the group of homeless people standing in a circle on the corner of the crossroads. They seemed to be cheering some activity on the ground. The crowd separated and Tyson saw a man who appeared to have four legs, with an abnormal hairy face, scooting his clumsy body around. He was repeatedly doing an awkward dance move for the crowd.

Rex hit the gas pedal and drove assertively through the intersection. As they approached an abandoned apartment building, there seemed to be numerous children scurrying around the ruins like ants. The children were appearing and disappearing here and there through halls and entry ways created by bombs and mortar rounds.

Rex smiled and shifted the van into second gear for the first time. Tyson, fighting exhaustion, shut his eyes and didn't open them until Rex placed his small body on the bed in his room at the Hermes Opal hotel. He tried to stay awake, but eventually relented to the jet lag and fell into a deep sleep.

The Hermes Opal was known for its high standards of service spanning the last one hundred years. Since they were a party of three, it made more sense to book two separate suites with a total of three beds. The adjoining rooms were located near the elevator on the sixth floor. The suites had no windows, but did have small vents near the ceiling that could be opened, allowing sunlight to shine through. Everything was very clean and odorless with lots of plush velvet material accents. The walls throughout the interior of the building were covered with leather wallpaper. The ceilings were just over twelve feet high and the bathroom in the wheelchair accessible room was a masterpiece of marble sculpting. Both chambers had brand new bluish-gray carpet. Everything else, especially the arched marble ceilings, were all parts of the original Opal structure built in 1915. The detail in the crown molding was lavish, and it was unmistakably crafted by hand. Only a few framed art pieces were placed on the walls. They were small, about eight by ten inches square. Each room had a safe in the closet. Everything about the room was impressive, which wasn't a surprise since this was the most expensive lodging in Bucharest. The new Hermes Opal hotel establishment was successfully exploiting the old Hermes Opals' architectural style.

Tyson woke up hours later feeling extremely disoriented. For a moment, the heaviness of his eyelids almost made him forget he needed to call Michaela.

"Hey Jack, wake up!" Tyson urged.

"Huh, what, why, where are we? Geez, I'm so tired." Jack took a deep breath and let out a long exaggerated yawn.

"You'll get over it, dude. Come on and help me," Tyson clarified. "I need to call Michaela." There was definitely an element of fascination in his voice.

"Alright, give me five minutes," Jack moaned.

"No dude, get up now!" Tyson hissed.

"Why do you always have to have everything your way, Tyson? Damn, you can be a pain, bro." Jack lifted his head and reached for his black framed glasses. "It feels like midnight, but it's sunny." Jack fought off the urge to crawl back into the nest he'd made. "Okay, I'm up now. Let me smoke a cigarette and then I'll help you!"

Tyson lay motionless and rolled his eyes. He despised being at the mercy of others, but at the same time, he'd evolved into a very patient creature over the past ten years.

Jack exhaled the last amount of dirty smoke and slid the greasy cigarette tip across the ashtray. His hands were wieldy from all the hard years of touring and playing guitar. This strength enabled him to squeeze and suffocate the burning tobacco instantly.

Jack opened the folder Tyson had prepared, found the piece of paper with all the phone numbers and details, and handed him the land line phone provided by the hotel.

"Okay, here you go, bro."

Tyson held the handset in his loose-gripping hand, while Jack dialed the number from a sheet of paper in the folder.

"Hello," Michaela answered shyly.

"Hey, Michaela, I'm here! Can you believe it? We made it!" Tyson was having a hard time finding words.

"Tyson, what is the room number?"

"It's on the sixth floor. Jack will be looking for you, and then he will show you to my room. I'm so happy to know I'll see you today, Michaela."

"Okay Tyson." She laughed quietly. "I am happy for this reason also. It feels somewhat miraculous!"

"Well, how soon can you get over here to the Opal?" Tyson inquired with confidence in his voice.

"I can be there to meet you in an hour, and I am very excited. Bye, Tyson." She hung the phone up, before Tyson had a chance to respond.

Rex and Jack sat on the rigid marble floor of the foyer directly across from the brass elevator doors on the sixth floor. Jack was dozing off and Rex had become quite restless, waiting for the doors to open. The seconds dragged so slowly that Jack was able to reach REM sleep, and he snored for over half an hour sitting, straight up on the hard floor. Jack opened his eyes, took a deep breath and glanced at his pocket watch with the anarchy symbol engraved into its silver face.

"It's been two hours. I wonder if she's even going to show!" Jack said while yawning.

Ten minutes later they felt the vibrations of the elevator car slowing and then stopping parallel to the sixth floor. The air in the foyer was thick with anticipation. Jack couldn't imagine the emotional mayhem Tyson had to be experiencing, while waiting back at the room. The doors casually slid open and a tall woman wearing faux-gold, stiletto high heels emerged from the brass-adorned elevator. Jack and Rex gazed at the sultry figure, while she tossed back the hood on her full length gray cloak. She removed her sun glasses and brushed a hand through her beautiful, shoulder-length blond hair.

The heels made no noise, as her leggy stride crossed the thick carpet, but when she stepped into the marble foyer, the stilettos sounded like a stallion stomping in freshly-fitted horseshoes. Her way of walking was balanced and smooth, giving her gait distinctive clicking noises with a captivating rhythm.

"Salut! You are Jack?" She asked.

"Yeah." Jack replied, while thinking how happy Tyson was going to be.

"Hi, I am Michaela. Where is Tyson?" She sounded slightly nervous.

"Follow me, nice lady." Jack said in a respectful voice. He then pushed himself up off the floor and introduced her to Rex.

Jack led her to Tyson's room. Rex followed them in silence, which was unusual for the talkative bruiser. After opening Tyson's door, they informed Michaela that they were going down to the lounge on the second floor for a few beverages.

When she walked into the room, Tyson knew she was the same girl from the dating web site. The photos he'd been looking at were obviously current, but she was taller and cuter than he was expecting. She leaned over to hug Tyson and followed with kisses on both cheeks. She was wearing an unidentifiable vanilla fragrance, which momentarily made Tyson forget his own name.

Michaela completely removed the heavy wool cloak. Beneath it, he caught a glimpse of a tight-fitting gray sweater and not much of it. Essentially, she wore just a short skirt and tank top, combined with the gold colored boots.

She put her hands on Tyson's thighs and leaned over.

"You have no idea how I waited for this moment," she whispered.

"Me, too. I can't believe I'm here with you right now."

She licked his ear and seductively ran her lips across his cheeks. Then she hit him with a big wet kiss on his lips. She pulled her head back and her large bluish-green eyes made contact with Tyson's gray eyes for the first time.

"Tyson, do you know that in Greek mythology, Hermes was messenger of the gods, and he was responsible for making dreams come true to mortal men." She stood up, brushed both hands through her blond hair and removed her tank top sweater, revealing her ample breasts.

He couldn't believe how much sex appeal Michaela naturally broadcasted. "Yes, I did know that." He swallowed and took a quick breath. "Hermes was also one of Aphrodite's lovers. She was the goddess of love, beauty, and sex."

Michaela released a sigh. "Yes, that is correct." She had a distinct Eastern European accent.

Tyson suddenly realized that this lovely creature he'd traveled so far to meet was the closest thing to Aphrodite he had ever seen, and at the current moment, this living goddess was effortlessly pulling her gray skirt up around her midsection. Michaela strutted around the room in white cotton panties and the gold stiletto boots. Her legs were long and her waist was tiny. The golden heels tilted her pelvis in a way that attractively enhanced the contours of her curvy body. She was gracefully moving through the suite, shutting and locking all the doors. Tyson enjoyed watching her secure their privacy. Then she sat on the edge of the bed.

"Come closer, American boy. I want you to take my energy." She positioned her hips towards the edge of the mattress. "Hurry, I don't want to wait any longer." He welcomed the invitation by positioning his chair so his feet were directly under the bed.

"Here, how's this?" Tyson touched her bronze skin. Her legs felt soft and had a strong smell of vanilla coming from the lotion or bath salts she used.

"Oh, this feels magical." Michaela groaned slightly and lay back on the bed. She raised her legs, grabbing at Tyson's head, pulling him towards her inner thigh. The scents and pheromones streaming from above caught Tyson's innate carnal interests, so he attempted to advance towards the source. At this intense moment, Tyson heard the faint noise of a key card sliding through his room's proximity reader.

He raised his head. "Did you hear that?" He could feel his blood pressure rise.

"No. What? Hear what?"

The door opened, making Michaela's mood change instantly. Her warm, soft skin became cold with goose bumps. Rex walked through the doorway just as Michaela dove under the down comforter.

"Excuse me. I left my money and key card in my safe next door. I need to cut through here real quick, to get into my room." Rex hustled through the adjoining doorway with a troubled look on his face.

"Oh, no problem, Rex," Tyson said gently. Only because he wanted to demonstrate kindness and understanding, while in the presence of this fine young lady.

"No. This is a problem." Michaela whispered to Tyson. "I will not tolerate any disturbances such as this!" She stood up and hastily pulled the heavy cloak over her head. "I need to leave now to meet my sister." She hurried towards the door. "Call me later this evening."

"Wait, Michaela. Stay here for awhile and-" His sentence was interrupted by the noise of the door slamming.

Tyson felt puzzled by her abrupt departure, but decided to file the misunderstanding into the "cultural differences" category and move on. He didn't know what to say and wished he had said something reassuring to Michaela.

One full hour passed and, as it was predetermined, Jack and Rex returned.

"Damn, you the man Tyson!" Rex spoke while he stared at Tyson from across the room. "That girl likes you and she's the hottest thing smoking in this country."

Trying not to spook them with his confusion, Tyson smiled and gloated, "Yeah guys, that's really her, not some old dude sitting around in his underwear posing as a chic. So, Jack, we can officially scratch that theory." There was an uncomfortable pause. "I'm sick of being all cooped up in this fortress," he laughed. "Let's go cruise around," Tyson pushed down on his titanium rims and leaned his weight back, creating enough momentum to pop a two second wheelie.

After spending nearly one full day in the luxurious rooms at the ancient Hermes Opal hotel, the entire group agreed they were ready to inhale the cold mixture of oxygen and diesel vapors outside. They waited at the elevator for five minutes, while the car made its ascent up the six floors. They got on the hotel elevator and pressed the scratched-up brass button with the triangle icon, indicating entrance hall. A few moments later, the doors opened, revealing the lobby's huge space, which now seemed to be full of people.

The uniformed doorman saw them coming, quickly he put his white-gloved hand on the old brass handle, and opened the door. Similar to a drone, he held it open, but did not move or look at them. He never took his eyes off the horizon in front of him. The tires on the wheelchair squealed for a moment while they rolled over the brass threshold. When they touched the cold, old cobblestone walkway, the ruts grabbed the wheels making it much harder to push Tyson in his chair. They decided to stroll around the entire time-worn Hermes Opal hotel.

"Hey Jack, can you believe how different the air is here on the other side of the planet?"

"You're right, it's really cold and hazy too." Jack said while making a shivering sound.

"Wow, look at the sky over there. The haze must be creating that surrealistic orange color." Tyson stated in awe. They proceeded down the south side of the building.

Rex said, "Keep it down guys. It looks like there's a dog sleeping in that wood crate on the walkway, up there to the right."

"Good idea, dude. Let's not wake him. I read on the internet that the street dogs here are totally aggressive and most have rabies."

The deliberate soft footsteps combined with the group's silence worked. They made it past the beast without disrupting its sleep.

"Man, Tyson didn't tell us how dirty this place was." Rex whispered to Jack in a voice loud enough for Tyson to hear.

"What, where?" Tyson snarled.

"Look at this cobble stone pathway we're on, and check out all the dirt on the windows and parked cars. Every surface is filthy!" Rex stated in his condescending way.

Jack cleared his throat. "It does sort of feel like the aftermath of a war zone."

"That's because there was a war, right here where we're standing, back in 1989. I guess no one has had the energy to clean when food and shelter are the main daily priorities." Tyson informed them.

As they rounded the corner and began traversing west along the backside of the Opal, Jack noticed four boys sitting on an eight-foot high, half-destroyed cement wall across the street. He gave them a quick thumbs up, and all four repeated the gesture. Jack smiled, but they did not. He slowly pulled his digital camera out of his jacket, held it in the air so they would see it, peered through the viewfinder and zoomed in. The boys looked about ten years old, with dark skin and brown eyes. They were dressed in an unorganized assortment of colorful, tattered clothing. The smaller one in the middle wearing a worn out yellow leather jacket held two large glass crucifix crosses to his chest. The boy to his right slowly lifted his left hand, making a rabbit ears sign behind his friend's head, while flashing a huge smile. The third boy held a dirty soccer ball against his orange vest and pulled his blue and yellow striped pants up to his knee, revealing some scar tissue that he was proud of. Then he spun the ball impressively on his left index finger. The fourth boy didn't move much. He only stared at the strangers with a cautious expression. Boom! The camera's flash went off. Suddenly, there was an unusual sound and the boys all looked down the street to their left. Reacting to the noise, they scattered over the wall, disappearing completely out of sight.

An echoing, clicking type of sound could be heard down the street in the direction the boys looked before jumping the wall. The sound, becoming louder and louder, was the clicking of high heels from several women strutting down the stone street. The foreign guys stayed in one place, trying to look natural and relaxed, knowing that these women would be in their sight within seconds. Four ladies came into view, walking shoulder to shoulder down the middle of the street, all displaying an elegant gait. Three of the women were around five feet eight inches tall, dressed neatly in black clothing. The fourth was speaking loudly and seemed to control the others. She was the only blonde in the group and had to be at least six feet tall, Tyson thought. The women saw the foreigners and, looking away, they passed by, ignoring them.

The three pushed on. Rex, the bodyguard, and Jack, took turns pushing the wheelchair up the back side of the Hermes Opal. Across the street, there was an opening in the wall, they pushed through and found a busy food market.

"What a good chance to see, smell, and eat new things!" Tyson was excited, but the two pushers were not, as they both noticed the outdoor market sat on a huge pile of loose stones. They spun the chair around and kept fighting the resistance of the wheels on the cobblestone road.

They spotted a pub on the northern side of the hotel. The sun didn't shine on the pub, because it was positioned in the shadow of the Opal. Another quick spin, then a wheelie, and they pulled the wheelchair up the four steps backwards. They entered the Gothic styled drinking establishment called Toxikons lounge and night club disco. It was located on the first floor of this six-story black marble building. This structure was more modern looking than the Hermes Opal across the street. The entire interior was constructed from some type of aged black lumber. They found a suitable table and sat, waiting to be served. The waitress had the same body frame they had been noticing everywhere.

"Hello, guys, I'm Roxana. What you like to drink?" She spoke with a lighter English accent than Michaela did.

Rex straightened his posture, scooted his chair forward and whispered to her. "We want some liquor. Let's do shots first and tell us what the local Romanians drink when they want strong alcohol!"

Roxana expressed amusement. "You want Tuica then. It is very strong brandy made from plums. I bring you guys some pizza and good German beers too?"

"Sure. What kind of pizza?" Tyson said.

Roxana glanced at the kitchen behind her. "Today we make the pizza with pork pieces, sheep milk feta cheese and ketchup sauce. You going to like it guys. I be right back with the Tuica."

Roxana returned quickly with their shots. "Narock!"

"Yeah, cheers to you too! Will you be my wife?" The bodyguard bellowed belligerently and then drank all the Tuica in one swallow.

She flashed him a huge smile and giggled like an embarrassed school child. "No, I am sorry but I can not. I will bring you more shots and beer now."

They ate and drank, feeling a lighthearted buzz from the plum brandy. They all agreed it tasted like grapefruit flavored whisky. Everything seemed to be perfect. Their arrogance started to emerge in the conversation. They unknowingly began to vocalize to each other how impressed they were with where they sat and how they were handling things. After about two hours they received the bill and Jack graciously paid it with Tyson's credit card.

"Let's roll," Tyson said.

16, THE DECLINE

Rex thrust the ultra-light wheelchair through the black wood front doorway, tipped the front wheels up, and then bounced it down the four steps in front of Toxikons lounge onto the frozen road. The temperature had dropped, and the effects from the alcohol, combined with the cool stark shadow of the Opal, made Tyson feel disorientated. The wheelchair moved easier through the rutted cold stones this time though, and the Opal's huge, brass front entry was just across the street and around the corner. They were all drunk from the beers and plum brandy and had lost any inhibitions they carried earlier. All three were speaking their brand of English loudly. They no longer felt like strangers, with the new liquid-encouraged comfort level. Rex stopped unexpectedly and unzipped his pants to relieve his extended bladder on the tire of a parked car. From his wheelchair Tyson took note of this behavior and decided not to make an issue of it, probably because his nervousness about this country was fading. He wondered for a second why he had been so insistent on hiring and bringing this lackadaisical brute.

That's when Tyson noticed the boy from earlier on the wall walking slowly in the shadows, down the street towards them. He still held the two glass crosses in front of his body in a rather symbolic type of movement. The boy unexpectedly disappeared through a hole in the damp concrete foundation of a burned up uninhabitable building about a block away from the three Americans.

The muscular six foot ten bodyguard twisted his torso and belched loudly and yelled. "Let's go get more drinks at the casino!"

"Shut up, dude! I need to go up to the room and call Michaela first, and then we'll go down to the casino!" Tyson shouted back. "I hope I don't need to remind you, but that's why you were hired to come here, so I could spend some time with her. Remember?"

Later, up in the room, there was only silence.

"Okay, give me that phone." Tyson extended his partially paralyzed appendage. "I think since I put this GSM chip in my cell phone, I'll just dial using my caller ID." He scrolled to Michaela's number and hit the send key.

"Hello," she responded.

"Hi Michaela, what's up? What are you doing?" His speech was slurred.

Her voice was subdued, "nothing, only watching the TV."

"Well, come on over!" It's amazing how doing shots gives you confidence, he thought to himself.

"No, not tonight," She whimpered.

"What? Why not?" He demanded.

Michaela took a deep breath. "You sound tipsy and I want to watch the TV. Call me tomorrow and we go for a long drive in the mountains." She hung up.

"We came all this way and she wants to watch TV?" Tyson whispered to himself. He hid his realization that something could be going wrong. "Do me a favor and get me nine and a half million lei out of the safe. Let's visit the hotel casino and take their money!"

"Hey bro, I forgot what we set the combo to." Jack said quietly, so Rex in the next room would not hear.

Tyson leaned closer. "You made it my birthday."

"Oh yeah, that's right." He successfully opened it and took nine and a half million lei out, leaving twenty million lei, equivalent to six hundred US dollars, in the safe.

They rolled down the thick red carpet in the hallway leading to the elevator. The casino was located one floor under the lobby. Rex had a look on his face revealing how he couldn't wait to put his huge, greasy fingerprint on the elevator's brass button labeled with the capitol letter C.

"I used to live in Vegas. Watch me show these Romanians a thing or two." Rex said loudly. He belched out a heinous odor that filled the elevator car. "Come on, man. Quit obsessing over this chick, will you? Plus you met her on the Internet. Let her go, man. We'll find some girls tonight for sure!" Rex winked with confidence.

Tyson exploded. "Look dude, you may not know this, but I've gotten to know Michaela pretty well for over a year, and I'm a little bummed because she'd rather be with a TV than me tonight, okay?" He lowered his voice. "I'll go party with you dudes since I won't be seeing her, but we need to remain together at all times. Please stay very cautious!"

Spinning around and looking down, Rex lifted his eyebrows. "Who do you think you are? My owner or something? I do what I want, when I want. I'm an independent adult. So, get off my back, man!"

The elevator doors opened on the casino level, and they pushed out onto a plush carpet. The casino down the hall fused black slate and marble together to create a three-tiered, large gaming area. A single craps table occupied the lowest level. Rex pushed the wheelchair down a ramp with three switchbacks. Jack followed closely as the chair's rubber tires squeaked across the polished marble floor.

They found a spot at the craps table where Tyson's knees could slide under. The top of his head was just inches above the padded rail.

"Can you see good enough, bro?" Jack asked in a discreet manner.

"Yes, but I don't think I'll be able to roll the dice." He raised his hand to his chin, demonstrating how far he could lift his arm. "Just like in Vegas, it's too high for me. I'll pass when it's my turn to roll."

"Give me the dice, you swine!" Rex couldn't wait to start gambling. "Where's our cocktail waitress?" He shouted at the silent, motionless pit boss.

The pit boss's wrinkled face glared at Rex's bloodshot eyes for ten seconds before he turned his back and waved a closed fist at someone near the bar. He turned back around to the table and flicked the dice to the hulky foreigner.

They ordered and drank more beer. Then they made stupid bets for about an hour, eventually losing millions in Romanian currency. A large crowd had formed around them to watch the high rollers lose an average Romanian's monthly salary in less than sixty minutes.

Rex was hunched over the table. With an angry expression, he glared at the smirking pit boss. "Alright, you illiterate loser," he bellowed, "I'll be back with more money. Probably more than you'll make in your lifetime!" Rex cackled with an evil kind of confidence. He stood up and asked Jack for the room key card.

"Here it is," Jack handed it to him. "The two of us will wait down here for you, so hurry up!"

"Don't leave the hotel!" Tyson uncontrollably blurted out.

Twenty minutes passed and Rex returned wearing his black leather trench coat, carrying a purple liquor bottle. "Come on guys, let's go!" He demanded, while simultaneously lighting up an oversized cigar.

"Go where? I thought you were getting more money to gamble with?" Jack asked.

"I did, but now I want to hit the strip club. It's only three blocks away. I just walked passed it a few minutes ago when I stepped out to buy a Cuban cigar. I found a better pushing path made from asphalt on the other side of that cobble road too and it leads directly to the club."

The tiny man in the wheelchair could not believe the level of defiance his "all-expenses-paid" bodyguard was shoving in his face. He decided to try the path of diplomacy and give in a little to the other members of the team. "Okay, let's go check it out, but don't tell Michaela about this when we see her tomorrow."

"I'll keep my mouth shut around her. Remember this too, there's no telling how many eastern European women I'm going to meet tonight!" Rex had to hold his stomach with both hands because he was laughing so hard. He wiped a tear from his eye, took a deep breath and bit the cigar with his teeth. He put the liquor bottle between Tyson's knees and pushed him up the ramp.

Jack was waiting beyond the elevator at the heavy glass door leading from the casino to the street on the south side of the Opal. He struggled with pushing the door against the cool breeze outside. When the wheelchair passed, he whispered, "Don't worry, bro, I won't tell Michaela either."

The high performance chair glided effortlessly across the asphalt path. The cold, humid October air didn't annoy them as much this time, as they jogged and pushed the three blocks in under five minutes.

Rex stopped walking. "We're here," he said and then spit a mouthful of tobacco juice from the cigar onto the path. There was no club, only a doorway with three capitol X's etched above it. "Yeah, come on guys, its right this way." Rex knocked three times and opened the door.

Jack pushed the chair into a small room with three flights of worn-down rickety stairs. The flooring had been ripped out and the dirt was exposed, giving off an earthy smell. Large tears and stains in the wall paper could be seen everywhere.

"I forgot to tell you guys, it's on the third floor." Rex announced and spun the chair so the rear wheels were touching the first step. Rex grabbed the push handles while Jack bent over and gripped both hands on the foot plate.

"1-2-3, lift!" Jack directed. They delicately balanced the wheelchair and took turns shuffling their feet, one step at a time.

"Dude, this is dangerous! We have all been drinking and I'm concerned about the weight of the three of us on this shaky staircase." Tyson pleaded.

The helpers gave no response. Tyson decided to revert to silence.

Once they reached the top, Jack lit a cigarette. Dance music was blasting down the hall from one direction.

"Where are we?" Jack said as he took the last puff off his smoke and put the smoldering butt out on the plastic wall paper.

Rex suddenly took on a serious, careful approach, slowly moving down the hall, tracing his finger along the ceiling as if the music was pulling him towards the door. He reached the opening, pushed aside a thick curtain, peeked inside and smiled from ear to ear. He made a fist, motioning them on and mocking the stern pit boss back at the casino. They moved through the filthy hallway into an astonishingly clean, upscale strip club.

"See, jerks! I told you this was the spot! I'll get beers from the bar and you boys sit here." Rex cheerfully shouted. He kicked the table and barstool hard enough to move them and positioned the wheelchair so Tyson's knees were under the table. "Sit here and get your money on the table and they'll do their little dance."

"I know how it works. Get me a Heineken!" Tyson had decided to enjoy himself, but still wanted to be anywhere with Michaela rather than where he currently sat. I could do all this childish crap back home, he thought to himself.

A dozen exotic dancers appeared on the main stage. The lights went down and the music became more dramatic. The dancers strutted around in second-hand lingerie, weaving in and out of the tables, hunting for the next customer. Tyson thought some were cute, but noticed most of the dancers had a strange smell when they pranced by. It was something like a faint garlic body odor mixed with dirty feet. They continued to drink and watch the girls. They tipped the dancers and chatted with them in broken English. The group dynamic hadn't felt like this since the Tuica shots at Toxikons earlier that day. The inhibitions were once again gone, and they were no longer concerned with caution. The girls were relaxing them, and the Romanian currency was gone in an hour.

"Hey Rex, all I have left is a US twenty." Jack said.

"Well, shoot bro," Rex paused and belched, "run back to the Opal. Here's my key card and safe code. Get me fifteen million lei," he shouted. "I'm going to spend it all so everyone will appreciate my good heartedness." Rex displayed a huge cheesy grin. They all laughed.

Jack stood up and said "If I leave, that means the group will be split up for awhile." He looked at his small paralyzed older brother for guidance. Tyson was absorbed in a massage. The safety of the group was not his highest priority at the moment, so he carelessly made a fist and waved it to his younger brother.

"Okay, guys I'll be back in like 20 minutes." Jack ran down the staircase and exited the building. He chose to run a straight line back to the Hermes Opal, bypassing the curved, longer asphalt route.

In the distance behind him, a car turned a corner and its running lamps provided enough light for Jack to avoid the larger ruts in the cobblestones. The car drove closer but did not pass him. He looked over his shoulder and saw an orange and white taxi cab. The driver was waving and desperately trying to get his attention. Jack stopped running and then walked over to the cab's open passenger window. With one hand on the roof and the other on the door handle, he leaned over and made eye contact with the swarthy driver. That's when he heard two pairs of quick moving footsteps behind him. Before he fully turned to see who it was, he felt the unmistakable chill of a steel gun barrel between his ribs.

"Go in the taxi, capitalistic pig!" The man with the gun said forcefully.

"What? This is a mistake. You must have the wrong guy!" Sweat started dripping from Jack's underarms. Instinctively, he pulled the U.S. twenty dollar bill out of his black leather jacket. "Here, take this," his voice quivered with fear.

The thieves laughed. One of them took the money and then they both got in the taxi. The driver revved the engine.

"You a lucky boy today!" He spit at Jack through the passenger window and they sped away. Scared and exhausted from the adrenaline surge, he ran back to the strip club.

"Hey, man, that was quick." Rex said. "Why are you all red and sweaty and hyperventilating?"

"I just got robbed!" Jack hollered "I really hate this creepy place! Let's get away from these scandalous strippers now!" He was clearly operating in panic mode.

Realizing that they could have lost him, the other two snapped out of fantasy land and headed for the squeaky stairs. The wheelchair was much easier to carry down since gravity was assisting.

Jack ran while he pushed his brother's chair along the asphalt trail. Rex followed, twenty feet behind the brothers. They made it back to the Opal in less than five minutes.

17. THE CROSS

Safely back in their hotel room, Jack washed his face with cool water. He crouched on the marble bathroom floor with both hands covering his face. "I can't believe you brought me here," he told Tyson with an irritated tone. "You put me in danger for a chick? Bro, what were you thinking?"

In the other suite Rex yelled, "What the hell!" He moved quickly through the doorway into the neighboring room and continued to yell. "My safe was open and half of the money is missing!"

Jack stood up, now visibly shaking, and looked at the other safe. It too was wide open. He counted the money and discovered that ten million lei of the remaining twenty million had vanished. "I can't believe this! What is going on?" He said through chattering teeth.

It was time for Tyson to exert his authority. "Listen up boys! Nobody leaves the hotel for any reason. Michaela will have to come up here to see me. And for God's sake, stick together!"

Rex snickered, "Come on, quit being a coward!" He slammed his bathroom door and turned the shower on. He reappeared an hour later, clean shaven and dressed in solid black clothing. Moving swiftly to his safe he grabbed his entire stash of Romanian cash and glanced around the doorway into the second room. Both brothers were mesmerized by the television. "Later, pansy boys!" He shouted and went out the door.

The two brothers talked for awhile, mostly about how they would have hired a different bodyguard if given a second chance. Tyson was getting sleepy, so Jack helped his disabled sibling prepare for bed.

Tyson slept soundly on the comfortable pillow top mattress until around three o'clock in the morning when Rex loudly busted in with some news. He knelt at the side of Tyson's bed.

"Man, you're not going to like this. I just saw Michaela at that Toxikons club with some big guy in an expensive looking suit."

"What? Are you sure?"

"Yeah man," Rex responded. "While I was watching, they went back by the bathrooms and he was kissing her neck. The whole time she was admiring her image in the mirror. I tried to approach her, but I got lost in the crowd and couldn't follow her from there. Here, give me her cell number so I can confront her. Shoot, now I'm scared!" He paused and then belched, but this time he blew the smelly air towards the ground in the other direction.

Rex dialed her number over and over for one hour, but there was never an answer. Then he passed out from all the heavy partying.

Tyson stayed awake the rest of the night, wondering why he hadn't sniffed out this trap earlier. He contemplated his next move. Finally, after hours of thinking, he said out loud, "I've got to get us out of Romania, first thing in the morning!"

The process of speaking forced Tyson's lungs to inhale deeply. Within seconds he drifted into sleep.

When he reached the rapid eye movement stage of sleep about twenty minutes later, Tyson could see a tile floor. For a second he thought it was strange that there were no colors, everything was in black and white or some tone of grey. He pushed himself into a bathroom to look for a place to empty his catheter leg bag. In the large handicapped stall, he spotted a circular drain in the floor. He leaned over and didn't see any feet or evidence that the lavatory was occupied.

"Yes, finally, I can do this without any help," he mumbled under his breath. Tyson hit the door lightly with the foot plate of his chair, stimulating the squeaky hinges into motion. Just as the door began moving, it surprisingly stopped. He pressed again and met resistance, and it felt like a human struggling to keep the door closed. Under the metal door on the tile floor he noticed a shadow twitch slightly. Tyson assumed there was a double amputee using the toilet, which was entirely possible in this battle-torn city. Thinking he made a good guess, he propelled himself backwards. He decided to wait, since there were no obvious options, other than the drain in the tile floor. Tyson had begun to doubt himself, due to the lack of any visible ambulatory device when the hinges squealed loudly and the door swung open.

His jaw dropped, his skin tightened and became littered with goose bumps. Michaela was perched in a crouched position on the closed toilet seat, wearing a black latex body suit. She stomped her black high heel boots on the metal cover and released a sinister sounding screech.

"Are you surprised?" She placed her left hand on top of her head and shouted, "Bah!" In a taunting tone. "Do you realize who I am?"

Still in shock and very scared, Tyson uttered, "mafia?"

"The mafia will do anything to please me, but no, I am not a component of theirs." Michaela slowly put one boot on the tile floor.

Tyson could feel beads of sweat pooling on his upper lip.

"I was very close with a high ranking bureaucrat in Nicolae Ceausescu's inner circle. He was the dictator who was taken out of power in 1989." She gracefully brought her other boot to the tile floor. "Even though these administrators were not so popular, they were still able to leave me a fortune in currency and high amounts of respect with the new government." She tilted her head in an unusually seductive way and leaned her back against the partitioned metal bathroom stall divider. She gracefully placed the bottom of her left boot on the metal divider.

"Aw, whew!" Michaela shouted in a piercing way. A glow of light appeared in her left palm. She reached into the light with her right hand and pulled out a pack of slim cigarettes. The glow disappeared quicker then a blink of Tyson's eye. She fired one up and inhaled the greasy toxins, than exhaled the carcinogen loaded smoke towards the ceiling.

"My husband, Mr. Gogoasa, runs the largest organized crime ring in Romania. Kidnapping is our specialty and we are experts at torture. We have done contract work for many foreign governments. My husband and I are a perfect match. We can both abuse the government and the street mafias when we work together. We are very rich from our activities, but our friends tell us we are demented for the way we handle our business activities." She flashed an evil grin and gracefully took another drag off her cigarette.

"How did you know I was in this bathroom?" He said, sounding unsure of reality.

"Tyson, I know everything you did on your visit. We ordered 24 hour surveillance on you. There are secret passageways everywhere in Romania. One of my agents informed me that you were slowly moving yourself towards this wash room. I went through this tunnel."

Michaela kicked a small, unnoticeable door near the base of the toilet. "Tyson, you are like the big fish we've been trying to capture for over a year. We know about the trust fund you received following the car accident that injured you. We even know precisely what the dollar amounts are today."

"Well, wait a minute! That trust fund needs to take care of my medical needs for the rest of my life." Tyson sounded like a parrot that spent too much time at his attorney's law office.

"You don't need half of that money, you stupid monkey! We were going to release you for two thirds of it, enough to buy a huge castle in Transylvania." She looked at the worn down tile floor and sighed.

"You were?" Tyson said quickly.

"Yes I was. Now I am going to let you go. The truth is, I fell in love with you during our e-mail correspondence. My husband will be rather upset that you got away, but if he knew that I let you go, he would certainly hurt me!"

"So you're going to let me go?"

Michaela took one last look at Tyson and turned her back towards him. "Yes! Go out of here before I change my mind!" She barked in her beautiful accent.

"Okay, you got it! Thanks for your leniency. Just so you know, I fell in love with you too, Michaela!"

She lowered her head and pointed to the bathroom exit. "Now!" She said, sounding more serious than ever.

He spun his wheelchair around and pushed the fist knobs on the rims of his tires with more vigor than he had ever possessed. He felt strong and tremendously lucky that he would be making it out of Bucharest alive and not tortured, with his finances intact.

Tyson felt someone touching his shoulder.

"Wake up, bro! Are you alright?" Jack said, realizing that his brother was sleeping uncomfortably.

"Oh my God, that was the strangest, most realistic dream I've ever had."

"It must have been a wild one, because you were moving your arms around and mumbling a bunch of nonsense."

"Dude, that was weird." Tyson said while rubbing his heavy eyelids.

"What happened?" Jack inquired.

"Oh, nothing. Never mind, dude."

18. THE ESCAPE

To complicate things, it had been predetermined that at 11:00 am. Michaela would be dropped off at the Hermes Opal to drive the rental van around for sight seeing in the famous Carpathian ridges. Having awakened before dawn, the threesome were able to checkout early. Jack had arranged for the rental car company to pick up the van at 11:00 am. The two hotel employees were fine with crediting the remaining four prepaid nights, but they suspiciously talked amongst themselves and stared at the Westerners, making Tyson very uncomfortable.

The shuttle to the airport was due to arrive at the hotel at 10:00 am, but was running late. The three men were anxiously watching for the shuttle when, At about 10:45 am, something unexpected happened. A black high-performance Callaway Land Rover with dark tinted windows, approached the front of the hotel. The doors opened and Rex verified with a simple nod that the man getting out of the sport utility vehicle, blowing Michaela kisses, was the same guy he saw her with the night before. They pulled Tyson behind them so he remained hidden from every person in the hotel lobby. Rex and Jack picked up their newspapers and covered their faces. This was the perfect disguise for the busy entrance lobby.

Michaela was dressed in black leather, which helped her blend in with everyone else doing business in the lobby. She couldn't hide the seductive way she ambulated though. It was easy to notice her moving in the direction of the elevator.

Concurrently, Tyson saw their clown suit Mercedes rental van rolling through the hotel's guest parking lot across the street. Yes, he thought, she saw it and now it's gone. When she figures out we're not up in our room, she'll come down here and see that the van is gone. She'll assume were driving to the airport. The Bucharest Otopeni

International airport, where we entered the country.

As Michaela passed by the front desk and headed for the elevator, Tyson could hear her name being called by one of the men behind the counter. She waved back and pressed her index finger to her lips, motioning him to be silent. Then she disappeared into the slow-moving elevator car, right as the airport shuttle arrived.

Tyson needed to get them going. "Okay now we've got around ten minutes before she's down here sniffing for clues on our whereabouts. If we load into that shuttle bus right now and go to this city's other airport, the Bucharest Baneasa airport, I think we'll ditch her." Tyson felt like his plan was brilliant and his voice reflected it.

Rex surprisingly stumbled when he stood up, and his speech was uncommonly slow and deep. It was well known that Rex never suffered from hangovers. He could go on a four day drinking binge and still fist fight like the golden gloves boxing champion that he was. Tyson found his sudden slurred language and loss of motor skills very peculiar. Jack began loading the luggage onto the shuttle bus marked Baneasa Airport. At the same time, Rex bent over to pick up Tyson and fell forward over Tyson's lap, landing on the cobble stone street. Jack quickly picked Tyson up and lifted his motionless body to the backseat of the transport bus. He grabbed the empty ultra light chair with one hand and literally threw it into the rear luggage compartment.

Jack yelled "Get up Rex! What the hell's wrong with you?"

Rex looked at him with half open eyes and said "That is a cool shirt you're wearing." He sounded like someone who had numerous lidocaine shots at the dentist.

Jack did his best to pull Rex up into the shuttle. It took a minute for Rex to regain his balance and then he crawled into the bus. His eyes were shut and a puddle of saliva was quickly forming on the carpet under his lips. Suddenly, Tyson spotted Michaela approaching the hotel exit through the Opal's front window, and he instructed Jack to hide behind the newspaper. They raised their disguises once again at the precise time Michaela moved through the brass entry way of the Opal. They lowered their papers and watched as she went directly to the empty parking space where the rental van had been parked.

Something was bugging Tyson about Rex's behavior. "Jack, hand me my medication box. I think I forgot to take my muscle relaxers this morning." Jack leaned back and snagged the box from the bag hanging on the back of the ultra-light chair. Tyson placed two fists forward to grab the box, knowing he took them with his orange juice earlier, while eating breakfast. Tyson glanced through the clear plastic top of his pill box that contained his daily medication combinations. "Oh, no!" He said in a shocked tone. "I was hoping I was wrong, but my presumption was right on, Jack."

"Huh? What happened?" Jack mumbled from behind his paper. "Tyson, duck down. I think she's back near the front of the Opal. This chick is freaking me out. Now, what's this presumption stuff about?" Jack remained totally motionless behind his newspaper.

"Look at Rex's fingernails and while you're at it, Dr. Jack, take a look up our prize fighter's nose."

Jack dropped to all fours and caught a whiff of Rex's poisonous smelling breath. "Yuck, what's that smell?" Jack examined Rex's finger nails and nostril cavities. He returned with his newspaper and sat closely to Tyson. "Green powder everywhere!"

"I knew it! That jackass stole some narcotics out of my medication box. It's that high strength green pill I take to relieve my muscle spasms. I've heard of junkies grinding this stuff up and either shooting it or snorting it to get high."

Just as the bus driver turned the ignition, Michaela stepped in front of the shuttle bus. She almost looked fake, with her perfect haircut, tan skin, dark red lips, and black eye makeup. She impolitely impeded the progress of the shuttle to create a parking spot for the Land Rover. She snarled something into her cell phone and slammed it shut, just as a navy blue Lincoln Navigator pulled into the spot Michaela created. The passenger rolled his window down long enough for Michaela to hysterically yell something in Romanian. Through the open doorway of the bus, Tyson clearly heard her say the word Otopeni during her impatient hissy. The Lincoln Navigator took off in the direction of Otopeni. Michaela still stood in the street, preventing the bus from leaving on its routine schedule.

Tyson took one last look at her and couldn't believe he still had sincere feelings for her. Suddenly the black Land Rover, the one that originally dropped her off, returned and was dangerously cutting across lanes of slow moving commuter traffic. The vehicle skidded to a stop diagonally in front of the shuttle bus. Michaela frantically opened the passenger side door and turned her head, seeing the Baneasa airport sign in the shuttle's front window. She turned back and yelled at the driver "Baneasa!" She jumped into the back seat and slammed the door. The sleek black vehicle made a careless U-turn and sped the opposite way of the blue Lincoln Navigator's trail, towards the Baneasa airport. The shuttle's brakes hissed and the driver carefully merged into traffic, heading north where the road sign pointed to the Baneasa airport.

Tyson started thinking out loud, "Here's our advantage. Even though we both know Michaela went to Baneasa, we also know that as soon as the guy in the blue Lincoln Navigator sees our returned van in the rental company lot, they'll have to assume we're not at Baneasa. At least we haven't bought any tickets yet, and it seems that Michaela and her cronies could get access to that type of information. We need to hide somewhere and get plane tickets about 15 minutes before our flight leaves."

"Tyson, it's amazing how you come up with this stuff so fast, and you're taking the same pills as him." Jack said, pointing to the sprawled out, odor spewing stiff at his feet.

"Yeah, but my body's used to them. I've been taking that small dose before bed for over ten years now, and the numbing effects probably wore off long ago."

The bumpy fifteen minute ride was uncomfortable for Tyson. "Oh, damn. What was that?" Tyson bit the side of his tongue as his upper body slapped the empty seat next to him. "We must have hit something." I wish I was on my custom seating system in my wheelchair, he thought to himself.

"Here." Jack grabbed him by the elbow, then pulled his paralyzed brother's floppy torso back into it's slouched over, seated position. "You alright, bro? We hit that curb when he stopped and you went flying."

"Yeah, I'm cool. Good thing I have this lap belt on, huh?"

"Exactly bro. If not, you'd be stuck on the ceiling, just like all that gum up there."

Tyson tilted his head up, "Ew, gross. Now that's nasty."

"Yeah, it is. Can you imagine having to pick all that sticky, bacteria-ridden, crap out of your hair?"

The shuttle driver frowned at them through the rearview mirror. "I back in two hours," he said and then exited the vehicle.

"Yuck, Jack, come on let's be serious. Cruise in there and see when the next flight leaves. I'll just wait out here with our snoozing golden boy." Tyson glanced down at Rex, still passed out on the floor.

"Allright, I'll be back in a few." Jack jumped up and disappeared through the airport's sliding glass door.

Tyson turned his neck down. "Yo, you odor spewing stiff, Rex, wake up!"

"Huh? What? Come on, five more minutes, mom."

"Yeah, you'll be begging for your mommy once we get home and out of this whole mess. I can't believe your drunken ass, stealing my medication."

"Okay, I admit it. I snorted one of your pills and slammed a whole pint of gin down at the bar."

"Really, when did you do that?"

Rex yawned, "earlier this morning, while you were still sleeping. I want to offer a full apology for my devious behavior." He smiled and brought his massive body into a seated position.

Tyson wanted to display his disappointment. He paused then said, "If I could make a fist and get up out of this damn chair, I'd be down there on the dirty floor kicking your ass, buddy!"

"Ha, ha, ha, you don't even know anybody who'd take me on. If I could get up, I'd slap your little paralyzed ass!"

"You're right Rex. I don't know any hit men personally, but my money will help me solve that problem." Tyson yawned nonchalantly.

After fifteen minutes of silence, Jack returned.

"I checked all the flights, bro and one leaves for Amsterdam in an hour."

"Nice, dude, that's perfect. Use my credit card to buy three one-way tickets. I don't care how much it costs!"

"Me neither, man." Rex rudely interjected.

"Shut the hell up!" Tyson looked at Rex. "You're lucky I can afford to rescue us like this, you damn jackass!"

"Oh yeah, since you got us into this mess, I'd say you're the lucky one. Me and Jack should have left your ass back at the hotel, little man."

"Come on guys, stop arguing. Now!" Jack grabbed Tyson's wallet and pulled out his American Express card. "Sit back and relax. I'll be right back."

"Oh, hey Jack, did you see her in there anywhere?"

"Geez bro, I almost forgot to tell you. I saw her go out near the car rental return stand, on the other side of this dinky terminal."

"Dude, no way. For real?"

"Yeah bro, for real. She jumped into that same Land Rover and cruised off. So, yeah, your plan worked brilliantly, bro." He smiled and touched his brother on the shoulder. "We'll be home soon guys."

Rex chimed in loudly, "this vacation sucked." He covered the disappointment by putting his large left hand over his brow.

Tyson rolled his eyes. He couldn't believe Rex still thought this was supposed to be a vacation. "Well, at least you get to go to Amsterdam."

"True, that's very true." Rex looked into Tyson's eyes and grinned wide.

During the next sixty minutes, the three of them checked the luggage, went through customs, and performed the laborious act of loading a quadriplegic and all his gear onto an airplane.

Jack was seated at the window and Tyson was securely held in the middle by Rex on the aisle. They sat for twenty minutes while the other Amsterdam bound passengers loaded into the vessel.

"I don't know about you guys, but I'm getting hammered!" Rex announced in his louder than necessary tone. "Come on, Jack, we're on our way to Amsterdam, man. The opportunity of a lifetime, baby! Let's get some drinks!" He stretched his neck around to look down the isle. "Oh yeah, there it is."

"There's what?" Tyson murmured.

"The beverage cart." Rex reached back and hooked his pinky finger on the cart's push bar. He reached with every ounce of energy he could find. The wheels squeaked, which alerted an airline employee. An older man, with a dark complexion and skin that looked like leather, appeared to assist the impatient traveler.

"Hey, you mon. Let me help you with that."

"Oh, okay." Rex pushed the cart towards him. "I'll take a highball."

"Sure you got it. That's five fifty, mon." The airline attendant spoke like a Rastafarian. "Anyone else?" Both Jack and Tyson declined with a simple shake of the head.

As the cart rolled down the aisle and out of sight, Rex opened his hand, revealing six miniature bottles of various types of liquor.

"I snagged these before that Jamaican guy showed up."

The two brothers watched Rex slam the highball drink. He then dumped all six bottles into his empty glass.

"You sure you want to mix all those different..."

"Shut up, Jack!" Rex said, prior to downing the entire cocktail. "I'm going to the bathroom before we take off. So I can say a little prayer."

"A prayer for what?" Jack inquired.

In a breath that reeked of liquor, Rex stated, "A prayer that this plane crashes."

Tyson closed his eyes. "This is so unbelievable."

Rex returned and within ten minutes he was asleep. Once the plane was airborne Tyson felt a great sense of relief. Rex was conscious a few times during the flight. Each stint was full of slurred unrecognizable loud statements. Tyson and Jack both had blank stares on their faces, gazing forward at the seat back in front of them.

After a couple hours had passed, the pilot's crackling voice informed the passengers. "We will start our descent into Amsterdam in a few minutes. Current time at Schiphol International is 7:45 pm and it's a rainy forty three degrees Fahrenheit, six degrees Celsius."

"Yuck, I hate Amsterdam when it's wet and cold," Tyson complained in a low tone. He had visited the city previously a few times under better climate conditions.

Jack responded. "Yeah, it's not much fun when it's miserable and freezing. Plus our flight to Detroit leaves at 8:00 am tomorrow, bro."

"Well, let's grab a hotel room at the airport. Forget that fifty dollar cab ride into the city. There's not enough time."

"Huh, what the..." Rex twitched in his seat, enough to stimulate a cough with an adequate amount of force to clear his wind pipe. "Um, not even close, man." He smiled at the fact he'd completed a sentence. "I'm in Amsterdam, baby! I'm going out tonight, for sure!"

"Negative, not enough time dude." Tyson said.

"Why are you guys so paranoid? Ya'll are acting like you should be leaving Amsterdam." Rex snickered with an odor that reminded Tyson of the smell of a permanent magic marker.

No one reacted to Rex's remark. There was silence. Then a slim teenage male appeared with the airline's ancient wheelchair. "Welcome to Amsterdam, boys. Are you on a layover or vacation?"

"Neither!" Tyson snapped. "Can you get behind me, Jack? If this gentleman would be so kind as to move my legs by grabbing under my knees, that would be great."

"Sure, um, that's why I'm here," the airline employee said with zero confidence in his voice.

Rex was not helping Jack with Tyson anymore. Tyson sensed his next move would have to include a gentle reminder about how they were both still on his payroll.

"1-2-3, lift!" Jack's voice was steady and calm once again. They easily lifted and placed the motionless body in to the less than modern wheelchair.

"At least I only have to sit on this cheap thing for a few minutes."

"You look pretty stupid, man!" Rex said loudly.

Both Jack and Tyson looked at Rex and then at each other, noting a significant shift in Rex's behavior. He seemed to be angry at something, Tyson thought. They unloaded the plane and Tyson was placed perfectly upright in his gate checked ultra-light wheelchair. Jack pushed the chair with Rex's massive shadow covering theirs, as he moved behind them up the jet bridge. Suddenly, his large presence was gone. Tyson noticed it first, and then Jack turned to see how far the drunken bodyguard had lagged.

"Whew, bro, he's gone!" Jack said.

"Well, where the hell did he go, dude?"

"Not sure, Tyson," Jack scanned the busy terminal. "Wait, there he is."

"Really, where?"

"You probably can't see over all these people, but he's running the opposite direction, towards the cabs. I guess letting him hold his own ticket was a good idea, bro."

"Dude, who cares about that guy, let him do whatever he wants."

"You're sure about that?" Jack inquired.

"Yeah, at least we didn't leave him in Bucharest. Whatever happens to him, I'm not responsible." Tyson exhaled much slower than usual.

Jack responded, "I bet he'll meet up with us when the flight leaves in the morning. I guarantee he's curious about the coffee shops and the red light district. That's how we acted the first time we came here, remember?"

"I hear you on that, dude. Of course, I remember. Now we need to find that hotel somewhere in this terminal. Do you see it?"

"No, not yet," Jack stood on his toes.

"Keep looking, dude. I know it's here somewhere."

"Oh, okay. There's a sign, Hilton Amsterdam airport Schiphol hotel." Jack said.

"Nice, that's where we need to be." Tyson felt relieved to see the sign for the hotel.

They went through the routine ordeal of ensuring that the room was handicap accessible. Jack pushed Tyson through the lush carpet to the accessible room. Finding the appropriate bed, he transferred him over and rolled him on his side.

"Dude, I'm so tired." Tyson could barely speak.

"Uh-huh, right. That was easily the biggest adrenaline rush I've ever had. Now, I'm so exhausted." Jack flopped onto the second bed.

"Hey, Jack! Don't forget to set the alarm and get a wake up call, too."

"Yes, sergeant, sir!" He paused for five seconds and stared at the ceiling, blurting out. "Will you stop trying to control everything, damn it!"

"Okay, whatever! I didn't really realize I was doing that. Plus you kind of froze up back there, after you got robbed. I had to call all the shots there for a few, dude." Tyson was trying to calm him down.

"Well, you can stop now that we're safe and out of that damn situation!"

"Believe me, dude, I'm going to be so mellow and humble the rest of my life. You'll be surprised, Jack!"

"Yeah right, bro. You always get in trouble."

Tyson rolled his eyes and shut them, instantly falling asleep.

The morning sun was the first to wake him, an hour before they had to get up. When he'd finally gone back to sleep, the alarm and wake up calls set off multiple muscle spasms throughout his 110 pound body.

"This totally sucks! Jack, wake up dude! I need to take my morning meds," he groaned in an irritated tone.

Jack got up and assisted his brother with the water and medication. Without speaking, Jack got himself and Tyson packed and ready to fly. They rolled up to the hotel's front desk and paid the bill. Tyson spun his chair independently one hundred and eighty degrees and Jack grabbed the push handles. He provided the forward propulsion needed to cross the threshold into the airport.

"Dude, isn't it cool to have the hotel in the airport? You know, it's so convenient and all." Tyson said.

"Sure."

It only took fifteen minutes to check their two bags, go through security, and find the flight's departure gate. At the gate there was no sign of Rex, but there was a long line.

"Excuse me sir, could you please tell me what this line is for?" Jack asked a man waiting near the end.

"Additional security check point, my friend." He smiled and covered his mouth. "It's probably only a bomb threat."

"Wow, I hope not. Thanks for the info, sir."

Tyson was able to propel the chair and himself through the line. He was so happy to see a smooth, flat surface again. It took twenty minutes for them to reach the front and there was still no Rex.

"Next please." The officer said. They rolled and walked up to the podium.

"Good morning, I'm Officer Hafiz with the Dutch government. Can I get a verbal consent to ask you both a few questions?"

"Um, yeah." Tyson said.

"Sure, why not." Jack replied.

"Why are you in Amsterdam?"

"Uh, well we're only on a layover." Tyson decided to speak up.

"Where are you coming from?"

"Romania."

"Romania, hmm really? What were you there for?"

"I was meeting with a woman in Bucharest."

"Okay, from my records here it appears that you bought three tickets at Baneasa in Bucharest yesterday, and three people occupied seats on the flight to get here. So, where's the third traveler?" He questioned in a condescending manner.

"That's a good question. We really don't know. He took off and we never saw him again." Tyson said, hoping the questions would stop.

Officer Hafiz chuckled. "That's not uncommon with travelers to

Amsterdam. I think that will do it. Oh, hold on, there is one other mysterious thing here. Please tell me how many bags your friend, Rex, was checking."

"One."

"Are you sure?" Hafiz said, firmly.

Tyson looked at Jack briefly. "Yeah I'm sure. I've been with him for the past few days and that's all he had."

"Please hand me your passports and ticket information. You'll both need to follow Officers Ismail and Khalid to our private interview area."

Jack crouched down to get the papers out of the bag strapped to the backrest of the wheelchair cushion.

"What the hell, we didn't do anything, Jack." He whispered.

"Tyson, shut up, just cooperate here for a minute. When you get all defensive and pissed off, it makes us look guilty automatically."

"Guilty! Jack, we didn't do anything."

"I know, just chill out for a minute, bro. Let's just answer their questions honestly."

The private interview area turned out to be a basic office not far from their departing gate. Officer Khalid spoke English with a British accent.

"Please make yourself comfortable. Would you like any water, gentlemen?"

"No. No thanks, Officer." Jack replied.

"Fine, then. Now, do you two understand the purpose of this interview?"

Tyson spoke before Jack could prepare a response. "No sir, but I'm dying to hear why there's any suspicion about us."

The now seated Officer Khalid leaned back and said something to Officer Ismail in a language Tyson had never heard before. That's when it hit him that these security men were Pakistani citizens working for the American or Dutch government. This language must be one of the half-dozen or so spoken in that country, Tyson thought to himself.

"I'm going to need to know what happened to the fourth piece of luggage." Both officers stopped moving and only stared at the brothers. Tyson could almost feel all of their senses looking for any type of response.

"Um, we only brought three, sir." Tyson sounded confused.

"No! The three of you checked four items in Bucharest. I have the receipts we hold right here." He said sternly. "Now you two appear, minus one person. This means we take his bag off the plane and re-screen everyone who bought tickets with the same credit card. So here lies our problem. We get on the plane to rescreen the three bags and pull the no show, but there's only three to start with, and that door to the luggage compartment is under our tightest security during a layover period. So, you sir, tell me what is going on now, so I can get this plane to Detroit on time."

"I'm sorry, but I have no idea what to tell you," Tyson said with a smile. "Is it possible that a tired or disgruntled employee in Romania is responsible for this mystery?"

"I suppose that's possible. What about this Rex person you're traveling with? What's his disappearance about?" Khalid inspected his finger nails while waiting for a reply.

"He's pretty much a bum junkie we took with us to Romania for protection. He drank heavily on the flight yesterday and left us behind to go see the liberties of Amsterdam. The only person he'll hurt is himself. He's really pretty stupid and..."

"Very well, then gentlemen, I'll need you each to identify your luggage. Please follow me."

They all approached the glass window and, at the belly of the plane, Khalid directed a worker by cell phone to lift each bag for thirty seconds.

"That one belongs to me."

"And that's mine."

"Gentlemen, please enjoy your flight and sorry for the inconvenience."

"Dude, that was really weird." Tyson breathed a sigh of relief.

"I know. They were really looking for something. Makes me wonder what they weren't telling us. Oh well, we'll never know what that was about anyway. It's probably best to forget about it."

"Yeah, you're right, Jack. Hey, do you see Rex anywhere?"

Jack surveyed the crowded boarding area. "No, I don't."

"We are now boarding small children and passengers that need special assistance," a female airline employee announced to the crowd. She approached Tyson, following her broadcast. "Excuse me, sir, does this wheelchair have a folding frame?"

"No, it's one of the rigid high performance types," Tyson stated.

"Well, we need to gate check it and either carry or haul you down the aisle in our skinny chair over there at the end of the jet bridge." Hearing her American dialect was very comforting. "Regardless, honey, you're going to need this gate check ticket. When you get to the aircraft, the baggage crew can put it down in the belly of the plane." She tore the perforated ticket and handed Jack the pink half with the bungee loop attached. "Here, secure it to your chair so we meet regulations while it's stowed. Okay guys?"

"Yeah, sure, that's fine. I can do it now if you like." Jack said

"Entirely up to you, sir. Have a great flight back to the states."

"Tyson, why are you laughing? That lady was nice, bro."

"Oh, no dude, I'm laughing because I was thinking about what this damn ultra-light becomes when it's placed in the belly of the plane?"

"Um, I don't know. An empty wheelchair." Jack said sarcastically.

"No, you dork. It magically turns into another piece of checked baggage... The missing fourth piece." Tyson closed his eyes, "I can't believe I'm the one who figured it out. These people are idiots. Can I have my cell phone?"

"Sure, for what?"

"I want to call Michaela and ask her some questions now that we're out of her reach." Tyson let out an exaggerated exhale. "Why don't you go see if Rex is around here somewhere."

"Right on, here's your phone. I'll be back in like ten minutes."

"Cool, thanks dude." Tyson carefully entered Michaela's cell number using one of his numb knuckles.

He felt that she wouldn't answer and he was right, but this time a recording of her voice speaking in Romanian picked up and then there was a beep.

"Michaela, hey it's Tyson, calling to let you know that we decided to leave Romania in a hurry. Some bad stuff happened. My brother got robbed. Then, Rex said he saw you kissing a guy at Toxikons. Was it really you? Please get in contact with me. Call my business number, because I need to turn off my cell during this flight. Good-bye." Tyson felt better since he confronted her.

Jack touched his brother's shoulder. "No sign of Rex anywhere bro.

I think they want us to board this bird now."

"Okay, dude, let's roll."

The trip home was uneventful, which Tyson didn't mind. It gave him a chance to analyze the chain of events, but there was no clear answer. There was only the question: what really just happened?

19. HOME AT LAST

When Tyson returned home, the first thing he did was check his voicemail and e-mail. He was dying to see if Michaela had returned his call. To his surprise, there was a message from Rex.

"Hey buddies, I'm not mad that you guy's left me. Don't worry about me. I bought a ticket for a flight over to London to meet up with some friends who are following my favorite Colorado local band." Rex coughed and then chuckled. "Anyhow, I'm doing just fine and thought you should know." He laughed again and hung up.

"Yeah, right. Where did he get the money to fly to London?" Tyson said out loud.

He launched his e-mail software and found that Michaela had sent him a message earlier that morning.

November 01, 2000

Tyson,

I am really glad because you called me but I am sorry because you did not call me on Sunday before you decided to leave. I am sure that if you did it all the misunderstandings would be avoided. When I hear something bad I can not help myself and always ask that person if it is true. I can not keep everything inside me and wonder if it is true or not.

Anyway, I am glad because we have communicated and no matter what will happen in our lives we will always keep in touch. I hope your brother is well and not very upset about that bad experience he had. That is so strange your safes were both robbed. I wish all the best to Rex too, even if maybe I should not. And yes, I did see him that night while I was in line to use the toilet.

I hardly have found time to come and write you. Since yesterday I have cleaned the house at least three times because we had a party. Last night I went to bed only at six am because I had no room to sleep. Some of my friends stayed over night and I had to keep them company.

Now some relatives came to celebrate my sister's good grades. It is very boring to listen to all the congratulations and see all the gifts when I know I won't get anything. Tell me about you. –Michaela

Tyson was surprised that she was still interested in him, while admitting at the same time that she did indeed see Rex that night. He read it again and stopped in the middle. His eyes opened wide, and then he exited out of his e-mail program.

He rolled around his office for thirty minutes. Through Tyson's peripheral vision he caught a quick look at the new girl next door out in the sun washing her car.

Now, how would Michaela know about the robbery of the safes? Tyson thought to himself.

"I didn't tell her and I had just concluded that Rex hit the safes to get enough dough for his flight to London." Tyson said in his service dog's direction. "This is crazy!"

His eyes became fixed on the new neighbor.

"Greta, come. Let's go introduce ourselves, before I make myself sick, trying to figure out what just happened."

www.ingramcontent.com/pod-product-compliance
Lightning Source LLC
LaVergne TN
LVHW011243080426
835509LV00005B/611